GW01191637

HarperCollins*Publishers*

First published in 2012
by HarperCollins*Publishers (New Zealand) Limited*
PO Box 1, Shortland Street, Auckland 1140

HarperCollins*Publishers*
31 View Road, Glenfield, Auckland 0627, New Zealand
Level 13, 201 Elizabeth Street, Sydney, NSW 2000, Australia
A 53, Sector 57, Noida, UP, India
77–85 Fulham Palace Road, London W6 8JB, United Kingdom
2 Bloor Street East, 20th floor, Toronto, Ontario M4W 1A8, Canada
10 East 53rd Street, New York, NY 10022, USA

National Library of New Zealand Cataloguing-in-Publication Data

Oldfield, Natalie.
Dulcie May Kitchen everyday / Natalie Oldfield.
Includes index.
ISBN 978-1-86950-961-3
1. Quick and easy cooking. I. Dulcie May Kitchen (Firm) II. Title.
641.555—dc 22

ISBN: 978 1 86950 961 3

Cover and internal design by Matt Stanton, HarperCollins Design Studio
Typeset by Alicia Freile, Tango Media
Photography by Todd Eyre
Publisher: Alison Brook
Recipes by Natalie Oldfield and Michelle Burrell

Printed and bound in China by RR Donnelley on 157 gsm Matt Art

NATALIE OLDFIELD

DULCIE MAY KITCHEN
Everyday

PHOTOGRAPHY BY TODD EYRE
FOOD STYLING BY MICHELLE BURRELL

HarperCollins*Publishers*

CONTENTS

INTRODUCTION

My love for food was instilled in me early on by my Gran, Dulcie May Booker, who taught me that food prepared with love was at the heart of every home, every day. My inspiration is and always will be my Gran, and the enduring memories of her love, her food and the sharing of these with others.

In this book I offer my own interpretation of the everyday, remembering Gran's lessons and applying them to 'modern' ingredients. The recipes are simple and easy for everyday people and everyday use. Like my own favourite recipe books, I hope this book's pages will become well worn with use in your kitchen.

You will find recipes for every part of the day — from new ideas for breakfast to share with the kids in the weekend to my favourite easy lunch and dinner recipes and, of course, my forever favourite puddings, which I can never get enough of! There are soups to share, loaves to inspire you to 'cut and come again', special recipes your children can prepare and simple yet elegant suppers to serve to friends and family alike.

The recipes come from my own family: Gran, my mother, my sister and me. They have been tried and tested countless times on the people we love and are ready for you to do the same. Don't be afraid to adjust them to your own taste, or to the ingredients you have to hand. A key component of everyday cooking is the confidence to personalize and improvise. The trick is to replace like with like. Starchy vegetables like potatoes, kumara and pumpkin can replace one another;

try lamb or pork mince instead of beef; replace a herb you don't love with one that you do; play with the textures and tastes of different cheeses; relish the colours and flavours of a variety of vegetables.

Baking is perhaps the most exacting category of food with its delicately balanced dry and wet ingredients and the magic of baking soda, powder or yeast. But, if you're a keen baker, try a blend of white and wholemeal flour when you make a cake or loaf, add some nuts or bran, use different fruits and spices, and as you become more experienced you'll learn how to balance your innovations.

Ultimately, I would love this book to inspire you to make some easy-to-prepare meals with and for your own family and friends and relish those moments of happiness and celebration that go hand-in-hand with the preparation, sharing and eating of food. Food and love are made to be shared, and experience tells me that both are best when shared every day.

BREAKFAST

CREAMED RICE WITH STEWED RHUBARB **10**

CORN AND POTATO FRITTERS WITH SMOKED SALMON **13**

BREAKFAST FRITTATA WITH COURGETTES, CHERRY TOMATOES AND GOAT'S CHEESE **14**

MORNING GLORY MUFFINS **16**

WHOLEMEAL MAPLE SYRUP SCONES WITH GINGER BUTTER **18**

BAKED BEANS **21**

GRUYÈRE TOAST WITH MUSHROOMS, BACON AND BAKED TOMATOES **22**

HONEY NUT CRUNCH WITH GREEK YOGHURT AND SLICED BANANA **25**

CREAMED RICE WITH STEWED RHUBARB

Creamed Rice
250 g arborio rice
1 litre milk
1 cinnamon stick
1 vanilla bean
150 g sugar
400 ml cream
¼ tsp salt

Stewed Rhubarb
600 g fresh rhubarb, diced
1½ tsp fresh ginger, grated
2 tbsp water
1 cup sugar

In a large pot, place rice, milk, cinnamon stick and vanilla bean and slowly bring to the boil. Reduce to a simmer, stirring occasionally until rice is cooked and the mixture looks like porridge. This will take about 30 minutes.

In a separate pot, bring the sugar and cream to the boil. Add to the cooked rice mixture and season with salt. Set aside to cool.

Place rhubarb, ginger, water and sugar in a pot. Slowly bring to the boil and simmer for 10–15 minutes or until sugar has dissolved and rhubarb is cooked.

Serve rice topped with stewed rhubarb.

Serves 6–8

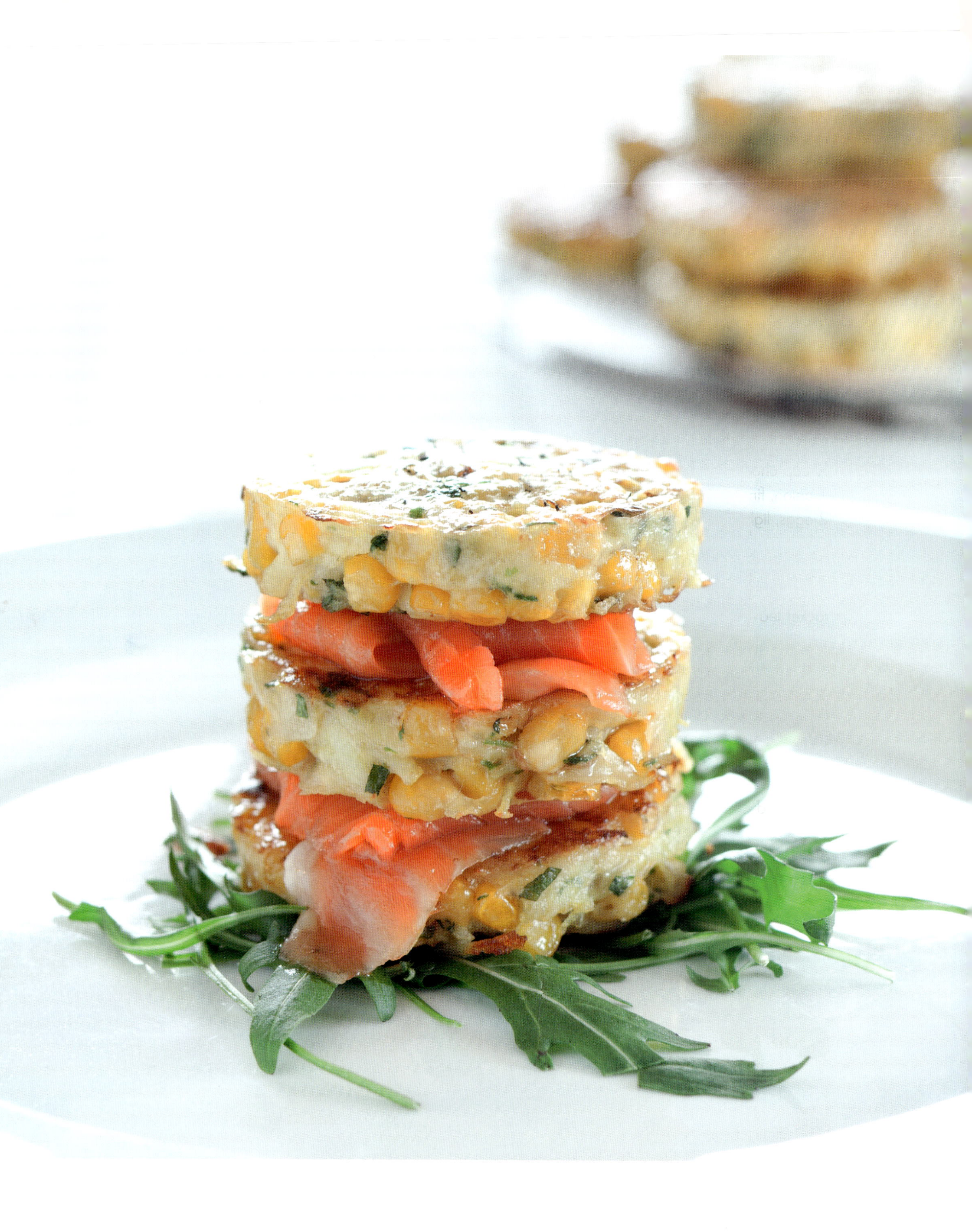

CORN AND POTATO FRITTERS WITH SMOKED SALMON

2 x 410 g cans corn kernels
2 medium potatoes, peeled, parboiled, then grated
½ cup chopped mint
½ cup chopped parsley
1 onion, finely chopped and fried
2 eggs, lightly beaten
salt and pepper
1 tbsp oil
12 slices smoked salmon
rocket leaves

In a large bowl, place corn, potato, mint, parsley, onion, eggs, salt and pepper. Mix well to combine.

Heat oil in a non-stick pan. Place greased egg rings in pan and fill with the corn mixture. Fry until golden then turn and fry on other side, making sure mixture is cooked through. Repeat process with remaining mixture.

Serve stacked with smoked salmon on rocket leaves.

Serves 4–6

BREAKFAST FRITTATA WITH COURGETTES, CHERRY TOMATOES AND GOAT'S CHEESE

2 tbsp olive oil
4 courgettes, thinly sliced
salt and pepper
8 eggs
1 punnet cherry tomatoes
200 g goat's cheese, crumbled

Preheat oven to 180°C. Grease a 20 cm baking dish.

Heat oil in a pan. Cook courgettes until soft but not mushy, about 3–4 minutes. Season with salt and pepper and set aside to cool.

In a large bowl, beat eggs, add cherry tomatoes, goat's cheese and cooled courgettes. Pour into baking dish.

Bake for 30 minutes or until cooked through and golden.

Serves 4–6

MORNING GLORY MUFFINS

2 cups standard flour
2 tsp baking soda
½ tsp salt
1 cup sugar
2 tsp ground cinnamon
½ cup walnuts
½ cup raisins
½ cup coconut
2 eggs
2 tsp vanilla essence
½ cup oil
½ cup water
2 cups grated carrot
1 apple, peeled and grated

Preheat oven to 180°C. Grease a 6- or 12-hole muffin tray.

Sift dry ingredients into a bowl. Add walnuts, raisins and coconut.

In a separate bowl, beat eggs, vanilla essence, oil and water. Add the grated carrot and apple and mix well. Add to the flour mixture and fold to combine.

Spoon tablespoons of the mixture into the muffin tray and bake for 20 minutes.

Makes 6 large or 12 small muffins

WHOLEMEAL MAPLE SYRUP SCONES WITH GINGER BUTTER

1¾ cups standard flour
½ cup wholemeal flour
1 tbsp baking powder
½ tsp salt
2 tbsp caster sugar
½ cup rolled oats
160 g butter

6 tbsp maple syrup
¾ cup milk
1 egg, beaten

Ginger Butter
150 g butter, softened
2 tbsp grated fresh ginger

Preheat oven to 200°C. Line a baking tray with non-stick paper.

Sift flours, baking powder, salt and sugar into a bowl and add the oats. Rub in butter until the mixture resembles breadcrumbs. Gently stir in maple syrup and milk until mixture is just combined.

Place dough on floured surface and gently press out into a slab about 3 cm thick. Using a cutter, cut the dough into rounds and place them on a baking tray. Brush the top with the beaten egg and bake for 20–25 minutes or until golden brown.

While scones are baking, combine softened butter and ginger in a bowl to make butter. Serve with warm scones.

Makes 10–12

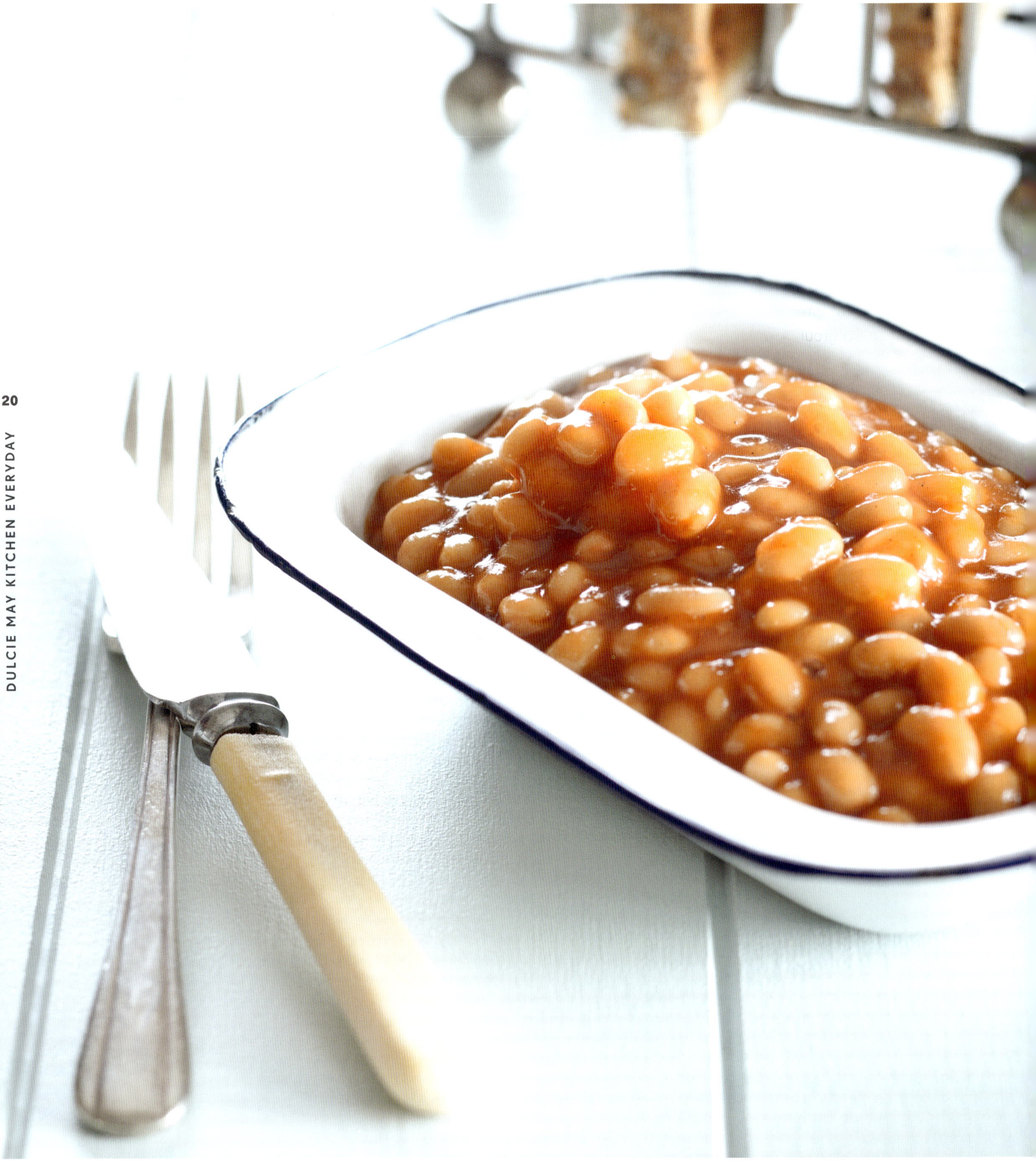

BAKED BEANS

3 tbsp olive oil
3 medium onions, diced
2 cloves garlic, diced
2 tsp paprika
¼ tsp ground cloves
8 heaped tbsp tomato sauce
1 x 400 g tin crushed tomatoes
300 ml water
2 tins haricot beans, rinsed and drained
1 tbsp Worcestershire sauce
1 tsp brown sugar
salt

Preheat oven to 150°C.

Heat oil in a large pan. Fry onion and garlic until soft. Add paprika and ground cloves and stir through tomato sauce.

Add the crushed tomatoes and water and bring to the boil. Simmer for about 20 minutes then blend until smooth.

Add the beans, Worcestershire sauce and sugar to the sauce mixture. Season with salt.

Place in a casserole dish and bake for 1–1½ hours.

Stir in some boiling water before serving if the beans are a bit dry.

Serves 6–8

GRUYÈRE TOAST WITH MUSHROOMS, BACON AND BAKED TOMATOES

Toast and Tomatoes
2 cups grated Gruyère cheese
½ cup sour cream
1 tsp wholegrain mustard
salt and pepper
6 slices bread
4–6 tomatoes, halved

Mushrooms
2 tbsp oil
8 rashers bacon, roughly chopped
1 kg mushrooms, sliced
3 tbsp cream
¼ cup chopped flat-leaf parsley

Preheat oven to 180°C. Line a baking tray with non-stick paper.

In a bowl, combine the cheese, sour cream and mustard and season with salt and pepper. Spread the mixture over the bread and place on the lined baking tray. Bake for 10–15 minutes or until golden brown.

In a separate roasting dish, place tomatoes and season with salt and pepper. Place in oven at the same time as the bread.

Heat oil in a pan and cook chopped bacon. Add mushrooms and cook until soft. Add cream and cook for a further 5 minutes or until mixture thickens. Stir through parsley.

Serves 4–6

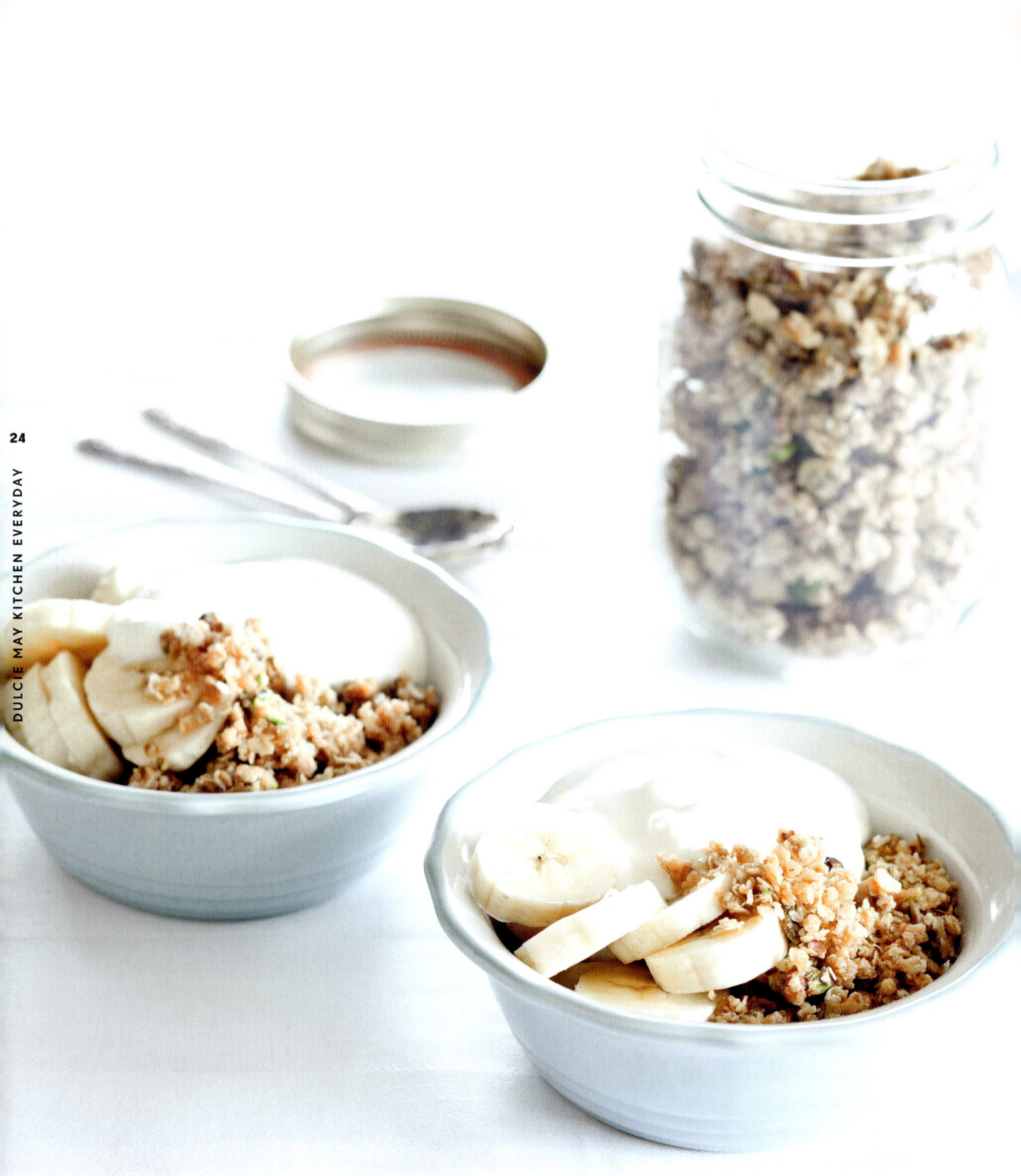

HONEY NUT CRUNCH WITH GREEK YOGHURT AND SLICED BANANA

¼ cup brown sugar
7 tbsp honey
¼ cup cooking oil
1½ cups rolled oats
70 g raw pistachios, chopped
500 g Greek yoghurt
3 bananas, sliced

Preheat oven to 120°C. Line a roasting pan with non-stick baking paper.

Place sugar, honey and oil in a pot and gently heat until sugar is dissolved. Add rolled oats and pistachios to warm mixture. Mix well. Spread over roasting pan and bake for 40 minutes or until golden brown. Set aside to cool slightly.

Serve with Greek yoghurt and sliced bananas.

Serves 4–6

MORNING TEA

QUICK CHELSEA BUNS

3 cups self-raising flour
½ tsp salt
50 g butter
1 cup milk

Icing
1 cup icing sugar, sifted
2 tbsp milk

Filling
60 g butter
¼ cup brown sugar
½ cup sultanas
½ cup currants
1 tsp ground cinnamon

Preheat oven to 180°C. Line a baking tray with non-stick paper.

Sift the flour and salt into a bowl. Gently rub in the butter. Mix to a firm dough with the milk. Roll out dough on a lightly floured surface to an oblong shape approximately 1 cm thick.

Cream butter and sugar together in a bowl. Spread over dough mixture with a knife. Sprinkle over fruit and cinnamon.

Roll up dough lengthwise. Cut into slices 2 cm thick and place on lined baking tray. Bake for 30 minutes.

Mix together icing sugar and milk. Pour icing over hot Chelsea buns and serve.

Makes approximately 8 buns

LEMON BUTTERFLY CAKES

1 packet lemon jelly
1 cup boiling water
125 g butter
¾ cup caster sugar
2 eggs
1½ cups self-raising flour
¾ cup milk
300 ml cream, whipped
icing sugar, to dust

Preheat oven to 190°C. Line a 12-hole muffin tray with paper cases.

Place lemon jelly and boiling water in a bowl and mix until dissolved. Pour into a square dish. Refrigerate to set.

Cream butter and sugar until light and fluffy. Add eggs one at a time, mixing well after each addition. Sift in flour and fold to combine. Stir in milk and spoon mixture into paper cases. Bake for 15–20 minutes.

Stand cakes in tray for 2 minutes then transfer to a wire rack to cool completely. Cut a slice from the top of each cooled butterfly cake. Reserve top and cut in half. Fill hole with whipped cream and garnish with a slice of set jelly. Use the reserved top cake pieces to make wings. Dust lightly with icing sugar.

Makes 12

KUMARA, LEEK AND SMOKED CHEESE SCONES

3 cups self-raising flour
1 tsp salt
60 g butter
¾ cup grated smoked cheese
1 cup diced leek
¾ cup cooked and mashed kumara
1¼ cups milk
1 tsp grated fresh ginger

Preheat oven to 220°C. Line a baking tray with non-stick paper.

Sift flour and salt into a large bowl. Rub in butter to resemble breadcrumbs. Stir in the cheese and leek.

In a separate bowl, mix the mashed kumara, milk and ginger, then add to dry ingredients.

Turn out dough onto a floured surface and shape into a square approximately 3 cm thick. Divide into eight squares and place on baking tray.

Bake for 15–20 minutes or until golden brown.

Makes 8

VANILLA CRISPS

175 g butter
¾ cup sugar
1 egg
1 tsp vanilla essence
1½ cups self-raising flour
1½ cups rice bubbles
½ cup chopped walnuts or almonds

Preheat oven to 180°C. Line a baking tray with non-stick paper.

Cream butter and sugar, add egg and vanilla essence. Mix well. Sift flour and add to creamed mixture. Lastly fold in rice bubbles and chopped walnuts or almonds.

Roll into teaspoon-sized balls. Place on baking tray and flatten with a fork. Bake for 10–15 minutes.

Makes 8–12

SAVOURY PINWHEEL SCONES WITH THYME BUTTER

3 cups self-raising flour
½ tsp salt
50 g butter
½ cup grated Parmesan
1½ cups milk
1 red onion, diced and fried
100 g feta, crumbled
3 tbsp chopped parsley

Thyme Butter
150 g butter, softened
1 tbsp finely chopped fresh thyme

Preheat oven to 210°C. Line a baking tray with non-stick paper.

Sift flour and salt into a large bowl. Rub in butter to resemble breadcrumbs. Stir in Parmesan and enough milk to make a firm, moist dough.

Turn dough out onto a floured surface and roll into a square approximately 25 cm x 25 cm. Sprinkle with red onion, feta and parsley. Roll up to form a log. Cut into 10 rounds and place on lined baking tray. Bake for 10–12 minutes.

While scones are baking, combine softened butter and thyme in a bowl to make butter. Serve with warm scones.

Makes 10

CORN, PARMESAN AND THYME ROLLS

butter, softened
1 loaf sliced white bread
1 x 410 g tin creamed corn
½ cup grated Parmesan
2 tsp chopped fresh thyme
salt and pepper

Preheat oven to 180°C. Line a baking tray with non-stick paper.

Butter the bread. Neatly trim off the crusts. In a bowl, mix together corn, Parmesan, thyme, salt and pepper. Put each slice of bread butter-side down and spread on 1 tbsp of corn mixture.

Neatly roll up each slice, buttered side on the outside. Place on baking tray. Bake for 15–20 minutes or until golden brown.

Makes approximately 20–25 rolls

LEMON MERINGUE SLICE

Base
1 x 250 g packet malt biscuits,
   finely crushed
1 tbsp caster sugar
1 tsp ground cinnamon
175 g butter, melted

Topping
2 egg whites
¼ cup caster sugar

Filling
1 x 395 g tin condensed milk
½ cup lemon juice
grated rind of 2 lemons
2 egg yolks

Preheat oven to 180°C. Line a Swiss roll tin with non-stick baking paper.

In a bowl, place malt biscuits, sugar and cinnamon. Mix in melted butter. Press into Swiss roll tin. Leave to cool until set.

Mix all filling ingredients together until well combined and pour over base mixture.

To make the topping, beat egg whites until light and fluffy, slowly adding caster sugar until mixture forms soft peaks. Spread carefully over lemon filling.

Bake for 30 minutes. Cool before cutting into desired number of squares.

POACHED CHICKEN, CHILLI AND CORIANDER CLUBS

butter, softened
1 loaf sandwich-sliced white bread
500 g poached chicken, shredded
1 cup whole-egg mayonnaise
zest of 1 lime, finely grated
2 tsp lime juice
1 red chilli, seeded and finely chopped
2 cups coriander leaves

Butter all the bread.

In a bowl, place the shredded chicken, mayonnaise, lime zest and juice and chilli. Mix until well combined.

Lay out a third of the bread slices and spread evenly with all of the chicken mixture.

Lay a second piece of bread on top of the filling, butter-side up. Place coriander leaves over the bread and top with remaining pieces of bread butter-side down.

Trim off crusts and cut into desired shape.

Makes 6–7 whole sandwiches

AFGHANS

200 g butter
½ cup sugar
1¼ cups standard flour
¼ tsp baking powder
¼ cup cocoa
1½ cups cornflakes
½ cup walnut pieces, to decorate

Chocolate Icing
2 cups icing sugar
4 tbsp cocoa
25 g butter, softened
2–3 tsp hot water

Preheat oven to 180°C. Line a baking tray with non-stick paper.

Cream butter and sugar until light and fluffy. Into a separate bowl, sift flour, baking powder and cocoa. Add to the creamed mixture. Add cornflakes and gently fold into dough mixture.

Place spoonfuls of mixture on baking tray. Bake for 15 minutes or until firm. Cool on wire rack.

To make icing, sift icing sugar and cocoa into a bowl. Add softened butter and water and mix to a spreadable consistency, adding extra water if needed.

Spread on cooled afghans and top each with a walnut piece.

Makes 8–10

GOAT'S CHEESE AND THYME CRACKERS

1 tbsp finely chopped fresh thyme
160 g goat's cheese, crumbled
120 g butter, softened
1 tsp salt
175 g standard flour, sifted

Preheat oven to 180°C. Line a baking tray with non-stick paper.

Place all ingredients in a food processor and pulse to combine.

Roll the dough out to approximately 3 mm thick on a floured surface. Cut into rounds with a cutter and place on baking tray.

Bake for 15 minutes or until golden brown.

Makes 20–25 crackers

CHOCOLATE PEANUT SLAB

1 cup icing sugar
1 cup chopped roasted peanuts
1½ cups cornflakes or rice bubbles
1 cup skim milk powder
1 cup sultanas or currants
½ cup cocoa
¼ cup coconut
250 g Kremelta, melted

Line a Swiss roll tin with non-stick baking paper.

Mix all dry ingredients together and stir in melted Kremelta. Pour into Swiss roll tin to set.

Cut into desired number of squares.

LUNCH

CHICKEN, CHICKPEA AND THYME SOUP

80 g butter
2 onions, peeled and finely diced
1 carrot, peeled and finely diced
2 stalks celery, finely diced
2 tbsp roughly chopped fresh thyme
salt and pepper
3 tbsp plain flour
1 litre chicken stock
2 cups shredded chicken
1 x 400 g tin chickpeas, drained
150 g snow peas, finely sliced

Melt butter in large pot. Add onion, carrot, celery and thyme. Season with salt and pepper. Stir in flour and cook for 1–2 minutes. Slowly add chicken stock, stirring continuously until all is combined and smooth.

Add chicken, chickpeas and snow peas. Bring back to the boil and serve.

Serves 4–6

POTATO, PARSLEY AND CHILLI SOUP WITH CRUMBLED GOAT'S CHEESE

5 tbsp cooking oil
2 onions, peeled and finely chopped
2 leeks, finely sliced
2 large red chillies, seeded and chopped
salt and pepper
50 g flat-leaf parsley, chopped
500 g Agria potatoes, peeled and quartered
1 litre vegetable stock
200 g goat's cheese, crumbled

Heat oil in a large pot and over low heat add onion, leek and chilli. Cook gently, until soft but not browned. Season with salt and pepper. Add parsley, potatoes and stock and bring to the boil. Simmer for 20–30 minutes or until potatoes are soft. Transfer soup to a blender and blend until smooth.

Return soup to pot and reheat gently. Serve hot with crumbled goat's cheese on top.

Serves 4–6

STUFFED BAKED POTATOES WITH PANCETTA, CHERRY TOMATOES AND CHIVES

6 medium to large potatoes, washed and dried
oil, to brush
20 g butter
¼–½ cup milk
200 g pancetta, diced and fried
¼ cup chopped chives
½ punnet cherry tomatoes, halved
1 cup grated cheese
salt and pepper

Preheat oven to 180°C. Line a baking tray with non-stick paper.

Prick the potatoes with a fork. Cut a slice off the bottom of each potato so that they sit flat. Brush potatoes with oil. Place potatoes on baking tray and bake for 1–1½ hours or until soft.

Stand for 5 minutes. Increase oven temperature to 220°C.

Slice the top off each potato and scoop the flesh into a bowl, leaving a shell 5 mm thick. Add butter and milk to potato flesh and mash. Gently stir in fried pancetta, chives, cherry tomatoes and grated cheese. Season with salt and pepper. Pile the mixture back into the shells and place potatoes on oven tray. Bake for 15 minutes or until golden brown.

Makes 6

PRESSED SANDWICH WITH CORNED BEEF AND COLESLAW

8 slices bread, thickly sliced
4 slices corned beef, thickly sliced
2 cups coleslaw
4 slices cheese
4 tbsp mustard pickle

Preheat sandwich press or frying pan.

Assemble sandwich in layers, starting with corned beef, coleslaw, cheese and then mustard pickle.

Place in sandwich press or lightly greased frying pan. Toast until warmed through and cheese has melted.

Serves 4

OPEN SAVOURY TART WITH PUMPKIN, SAGE AND COTTAGE CHEESE

Pastry
2 cups standard flour
100 g butter
2 egg yolks
30–40 ml cold water

Filling
400 g pumpkin, diced and roasted
500 g cottage cheese
15–20 sage leaves
1½ cups grated Parmesan
salt and pepper
2 tbsp milk

Preheat oven to 200°C. Line a baking tray with non-stick paper.

Place flour in a bowl, add butter and rub until the mixture resembles breadcrumbs. Add egg yolks and water and mix to a stiff dough. Refrigerate for 30 minutes.

Place pumpkin, cottage cheese, sage leaves and 1 cup of grated Parmesan in a bowl and very gently fold together. Season with salt and pepper.

Roll out pastry on a lightly floured surface to form a large circle 3 mm thick and transfer to baking tray.

Place pumpkin filling on pastry leaving a 3 cm edge. Fold edge over top of pumpkin mixture. Brush pastry with milk. Sprinkle with remaining Parmesan and bake for 30–40 minutes or until golden brown.

Serves 6

QUICHES WITH CARAMELIZED ONION, MOZZARELLA AND BROCCOLI

2 sheets ready rolled shortcrust pastry
8 tbsp caramelized onion
1 x 250 g tub mozzarella, sliced into eight
8 florets broccoli, blanched
1 cup cream
2 eggs
1 egg yolk
salt and pepper
pinch of grated nutmeg

Preheat oven to 180°C. Grease eight 11 cm x 11 cm pie tins.

Cut each pastry sheet into four and line tins with pastry. Blind-bake pastry cases for 20–25 minutes, until the pastry is dry and slightly golden. (I use foil and rice to bake blind.) Leave to cool slightly.

In each pastry case, place 1 tablespoon of caramelized onion, 1 slice of mozzarella and 1 floret of broccoli.

In a bowl, mix together cream, eggs, egg yolk, salt, pepper and nutmeg. Mix to combine. Pour evenly between the pie tins.

Bake for 15–20 minutes or until filling has set and is slightly golden.

Serves 8

ROASTED PARSNIP, LENTIL AND MINT SALAD

1 small red onion, thinly sliced
3 tbsp red wine vinegar
1 tsp salt
4 tbsp olive oil
4 tbsp chopped fresh mint
1 tbsp roughly chopped fresh thyme leaves
3 large parsnips, peeled, sliced and roasted
1 x 250 g tin brown lentils, drained
130 g baby spinach leaves
70 g hazelnuts, roasted and chopped
200 g goat's cheese, crumbled

Place red onion in a medium bowl. Pour over red wine vinegar and salt. Stir and set aside for 10 minutes.

Add olive oil, mint, thyme, parsnip, lentils and baby spinach to the red onion. Gently mix together and transfer to desired serving dish.

Sprinkle with hazelnuts and crumbled goat's cheese. Serve immediately.

Serves 4–6

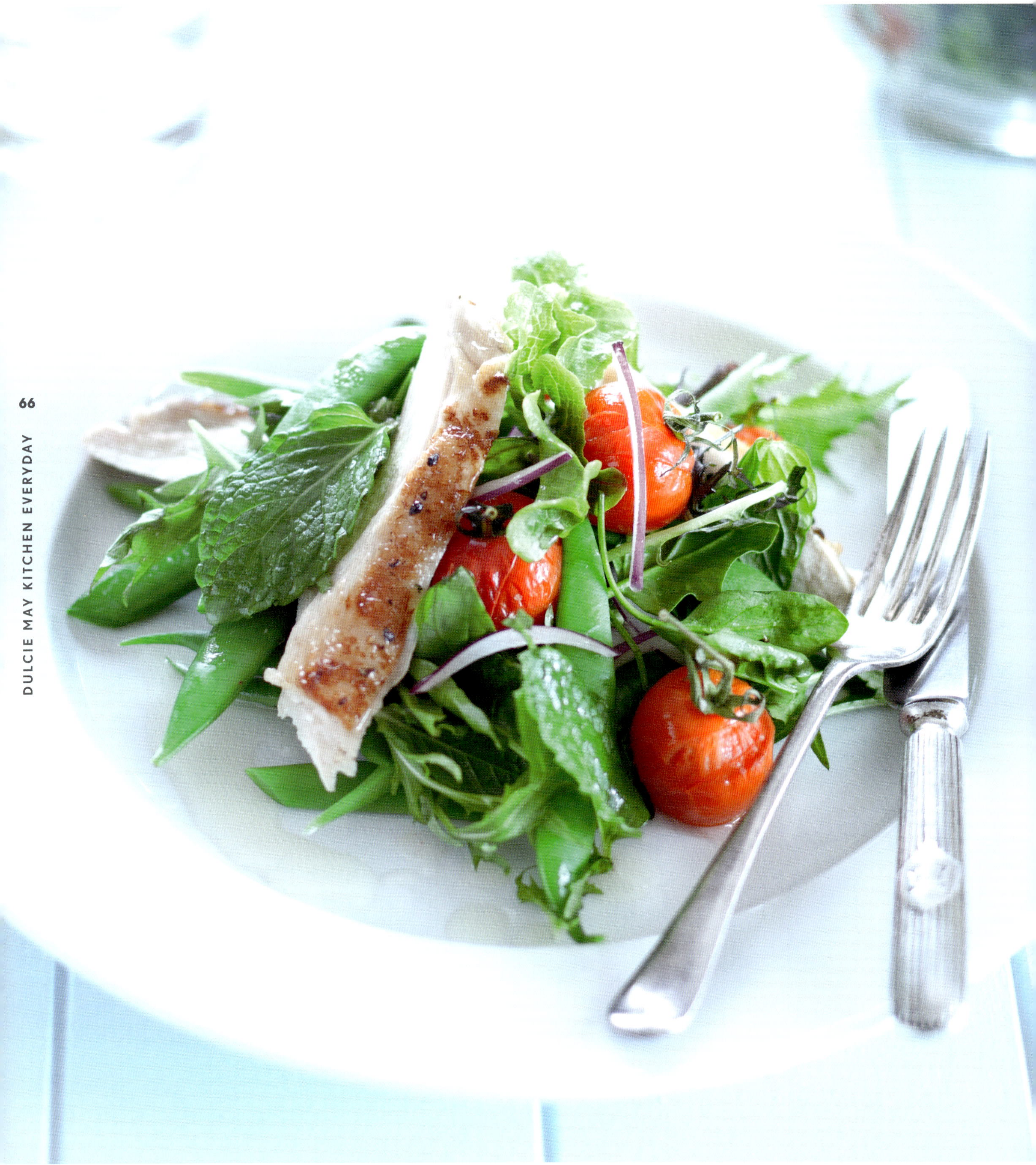

CHICKEN, ROASTED TOMATO AND BEAN SALAD

2 chicken breasts
salt and pepper
1 tbsp cooking oil
120 g mesclun
1 cup mint leaves
zest of 1 lime
150 g snow peas, blanched
400 g green beans, topped and blanched
12 vine tomatoes, roasted

Dressing
juice of 1 lime
$\frac{1}{8}$ cup sunflower oil
1 tsp peanut oil
$\frac{1}{4}$ tsp salt
1 tbsp sugar

Slice chicken breast in half horizontally. Season with salt and pepper. Heat oil in pan and fry chicken breast until cooked through. Allow to cool to room temperature, then slice into thin strips.

In a large bowl, place mesclun, mint, lime zest, snow peas and green beans and toss to combine.

For the dressing, place all ingredients in a jar and shake until well combined.

Transfer salad mix to a serving dish and layer with chicken and roasted tomatoes. Lastly, pour over dressing.

Serves 4–6

POACHED CHICKEN

4 small chicken breasts
1 bunch coriander
3 cm fresh ginger, sliced
1 lime, thinly sliced
2 spring onions, roughly chopped

Place chicken in the bottom of a large pot in a tight single layer. Cover chicken with water, adding enough so it is 4 cm above the chicken. Add coriander, ginger, lime and spring onion.

Cover and bring to the boil. Simmer for 5 minutes.

Remove from heat and cool without removing lid.

Once cooled to room temperature place in fridge, leaving in the poaching liquid until required.

Serves 4

SPINACH AND MUSHROOM ROULADE

1 x 350 g bag frozen spinach
1 tbsp butter
4 eggs, separated
½ tsp salt
1 tsp ground black pepper
¼ cup grated Parmesan

Filling
1 tbsp butter
1½ cups sliced mushrooms
1 tbsp flour
⅔ cup milk
⅛ tsp nutmeg
salt and pepper

Preheat oven to 180°C. Line a Swiss roll tin with non-stick baking paper.

Place spinach in a medium pot with butter and cook until soft. Drain spinach well and place in a large mixing bowl. Add egg yolks and mix well. Season with salt and pepper.

Whisk egg whites until soft peaks form. Fold egg whites into spinach mixture and spoon mixture into Swiss roll tin. Sprinkle over Parmesan and bake for 10–15 minutes.

Meanwhile, heat butter for filling in a medium pot, add mushrooms and cook until softened. Add flour and cook, stirring for 1 minute. Slowly pour in milk, stirring continuously until sauce has thickened. Add nutmeg and season with salt and pepper.

Remove roulade from oven and gently tip onto a sheet of waxed paper. Spread the mushroom filling on surface and gently roll up roulade. Cut into thick slices and serve immediately.

Serves 4–6

TOMATO AND HERB SALAD

1 kg mixed tomatoes, roughly chopped
1 small red onion, very thinly sliced
zest of 1 lemon
1 tbsp each chopped flat-leaf parsley, mint and coriander
1 tbsp capers, chopped
salt and pepper
olive oil

Place tomatoes, red onion, lemon zest, fresh herbs and capers in a large mixing bowl. Gently fold to combine and season with salt and pepper. Arrange salad on serving platter and drizzle with olive oil.

Serves 4

BALSAMIC ROASTED VEGETABLE AND MOZZARELLA SCONE PIZZA

Topping
2 cups butternut pumpkin, peeled and diced
2 red onions, sliced
1 red capsicum, sliced
olive oil
salt and pepper
1 large courgette, sliced
2 tbsp balsamic vinegar
1 x 400 g tin crushed tomatoes
200 g fresh mozzarella, torn into small pieces
1 cup rocket leaves

Base
2 cups white floour
1 cup wholemeal flour
2 tsp baking powder
1 tsp salt
100 g butter
1 cup milk

Preheat oven to 180°C. Line a large roasting dish with baking paper. Place pumpkin, onion and capsicum together in the roasting dish, toss vegetables with oil and season with salt and pepper. Roast for 10 minutes. Remove roasting dish from oven and add courgette. Return roasting dish to oven and roast for a further 10 minutes. Remove from oven and toss through balsamic vinegar.

Turn oven up to 220°C. Line a baking tray with non-stick paper.

To make base, sift together flours, baking powder and salt. Rub in butter to resemble fine breadcrumbs. Add milk and mix to form a soft dough. Roll out into a large square, approximately 30 cm x 30 cm, and place on baking tray.

Spread base with crushed tomatoes, then top with roast vegetables and torn mozzarella. Return to oven and bake for 15–20 minutes or until golden. Scatter over rocket leaves and drizzle with olive oil to serve.

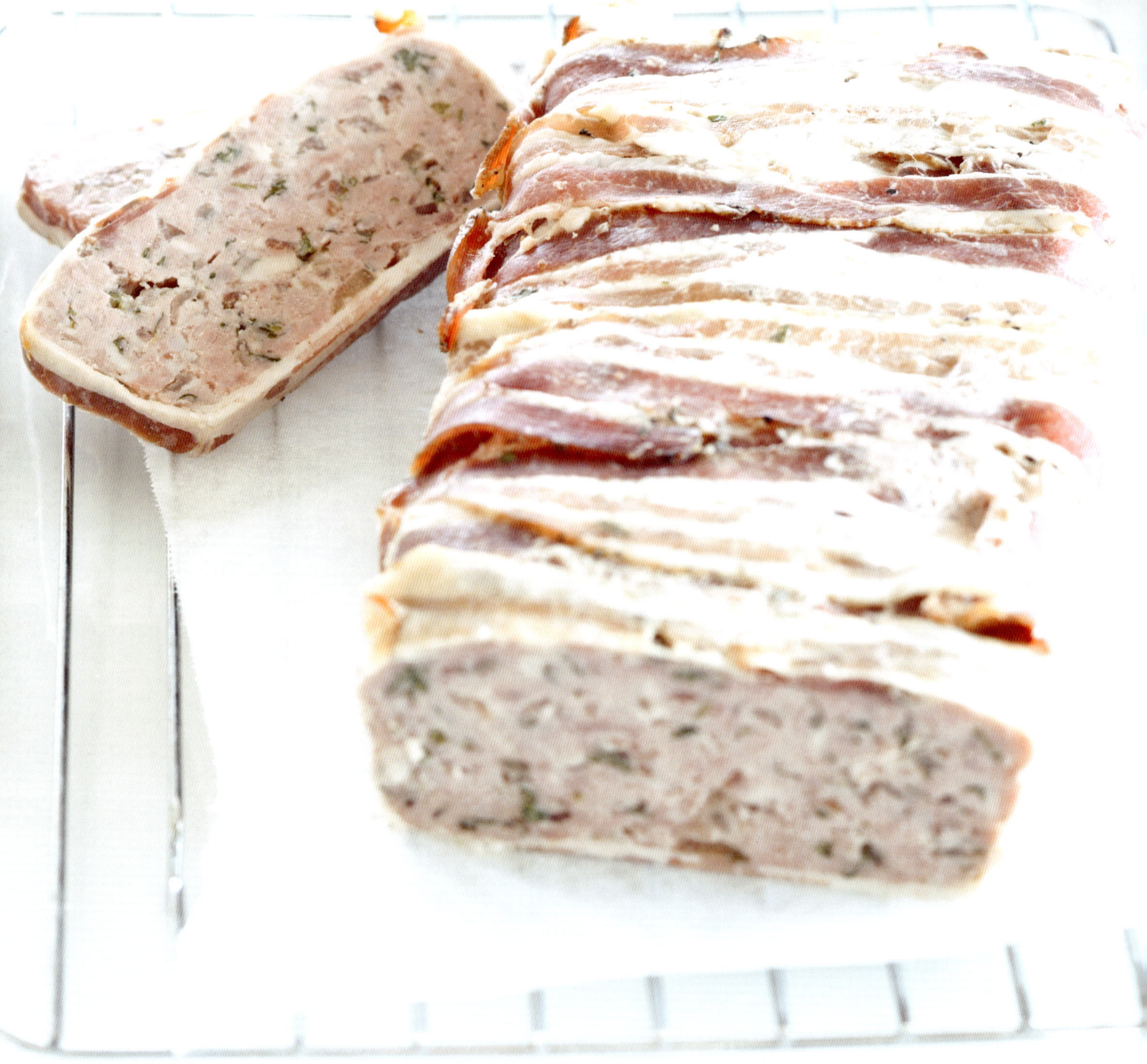

QUICK PORK AND HERB TERRINE

8–12 slices streaky bacon
1 tbsp oil
1 onion, finely diced
2 tbsp brandy
500 g pork mince
1 tsp grated nutmeg
1 tbsp fresh chopped fresh thyme leaves
salt and pepper

Preheat oven to 180°C. Line a loaf tin with streaky bacon, leaving enough overhanging the sides to enclose the top.

Heat oil in a frying pan, add onion and cook until soft. Add brandy and simmer until liquid has evaporated. Transfer to a bowl and cool.

Add mince, nutmeg and thyme to onion mixture and season with salt and pepper. Mix until well combined. Pack mixture into loaf tin, pressing down well. Cover the top with overhanging bacon.

Cover loaf tin with foil and place in roasting pan. Pour in enough boiling water to come halfway up the side of loaf tin. Bake for 1 hour.

Remove foil and bake for a further 10 minutes or until bacon is crispy on the top. Remove terrine from roasting pan and set aside to cool. Drain off any excess juices. Place in fridge until cold.

Serves 6–8

COOKING FOR KIDS

CHOCOLATE CRACKLES

12 paper cases
4 tbsp Kremelta
200 g dark chocolate, broken into squares
4 cups rice bubbles
hundreds and thousands

Line a muffin tray with 12 paper cases.

Place Kremelta in a large pot and melt over medium heat. Stir in the chocolate and mix until smooth.

Add the rice bubbles and mix until they are completely covered with chocolate.

Spoon the chocolate crackle mixture into the paper cases. Top with hundreds and thousands. Refrigerate until set.

Makes 12

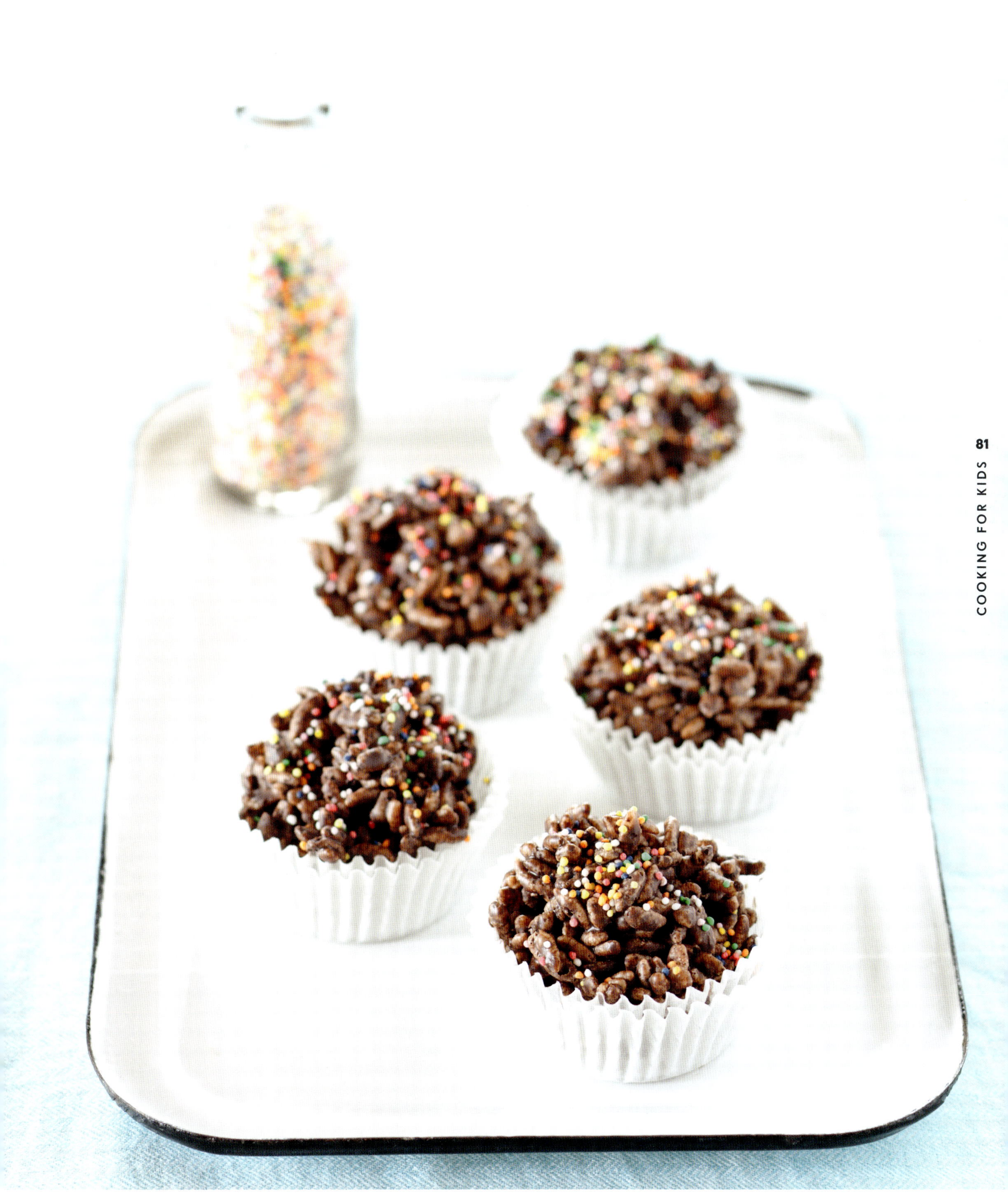

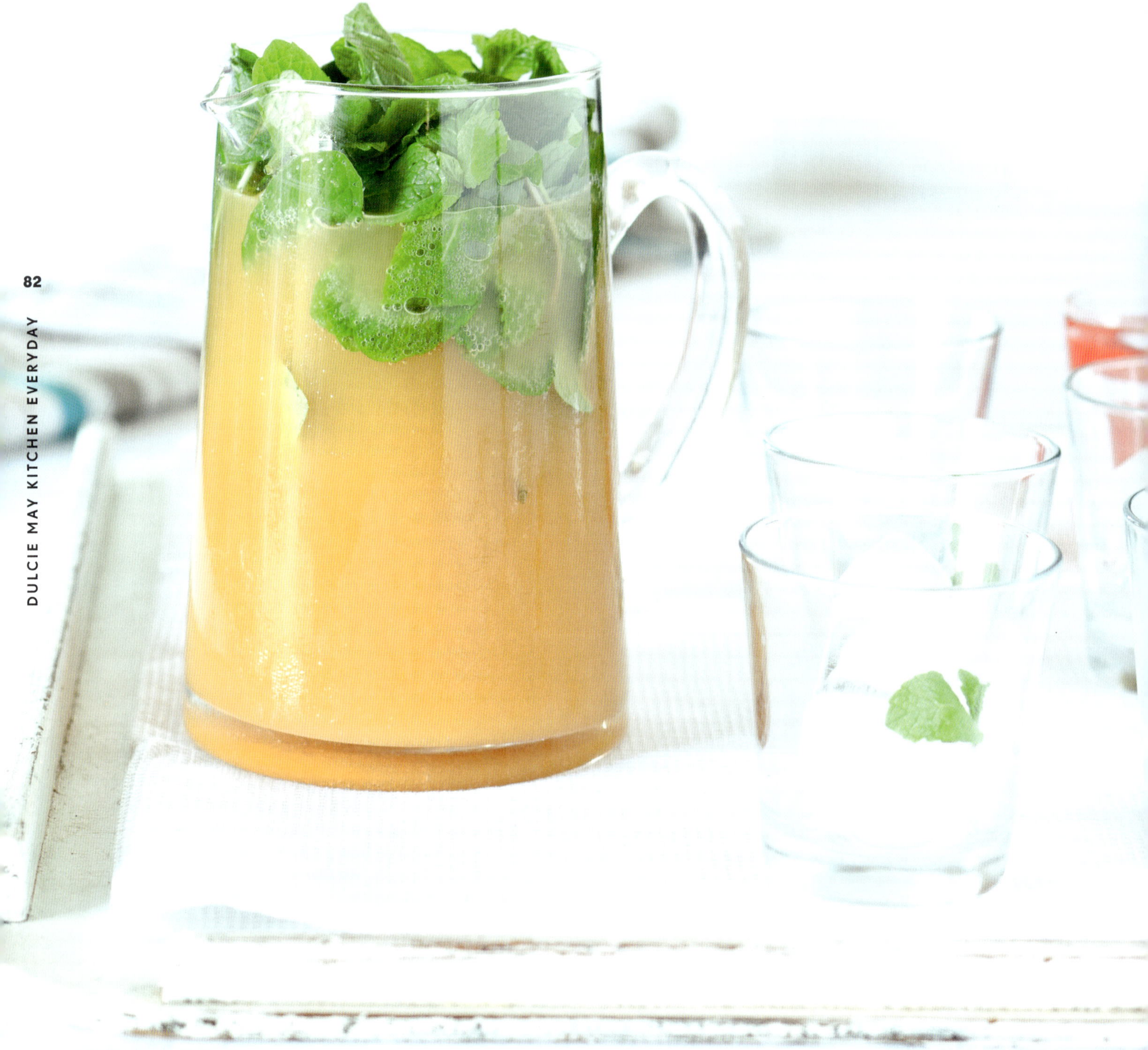

FRUIT PUNCH

600 ml apple juice
600 ml orange juice
600 ml pineapple juice
250 ml Rose's lime cordial
600 ml ginger ale
600 ml Lemon & Paeroa
fresh mint
blocks of ice

Mix all liquids together in a large bowl. Ladle into jug and top with fresh mint and ice.

Makes 3¼ litres

BREAD CASE SALMON PIES

12 slices white bread
50 g butter, chopped
¼ cup plain flour
1½ cups milk
1 x 415 g tin pink salmon, drained and flaked
2 tbsp chopped chives
salt and pepper
½ cup grated cheese

Preheat oven to 180°C. Lightly grease a 12-hole muffin tray.

Trim crusts from bread. Press into tray holes. Cook for 15 minutes or until edges are crisp and golden.

Melt butter in a saucepan over low heat. Add flour. Cook, stirring, until bubbling. Slowly add milk, whisking until combined. Bring to the boil. Whisk for 2 minutes or until thick. Remove from heat. Stir in flaked salmon and chives. Season with salt and pepper and spoon into bread cases. Top with cheese and place in the oven for a further 15 minutes.

Makes 12

CHICKEN NUGGETS

2 cups toasted breadcrumbs
1½ cups finely grated Parmesan
2 eggs
⅔ cup standard flour
4 chicken breast fillets, cut into nugget-sized pieces
cooking oil, to brush
1 cup mayonnaise
2 tsp basil pesto

Preheat oven to 180°C. Line a baking tray with non-stick paper.

In a large bowl, mix together breadcrumbs and Parmesan. Transfer to a large plate.
Beat eggs in a small bowl and place flour on a large plate.

Dip chicken pieces in flour, coating well, and then in egg and finally in breadcrumb mix.

Place nuggets on baking tray and brush each side with a generous amount of oil.
Bake for 15–20 minutes or until cooked through.

Mix mayonnaise and basil pesto in a bowl until combined. Serve nuggets with mayo mix.

Serves 6–8

PINEAPPLE AND BANANA ICE BLOCKS

½ pineapple, peeled, cored and cut into chunks
1 banana, peeled and cut into chunks
¼ cup lemon juice

Place all ingredients in a blender and mix until it forms a smooth purée.

Pour mix into ice-block moulds. Freeze overnight.

Makes 10–12

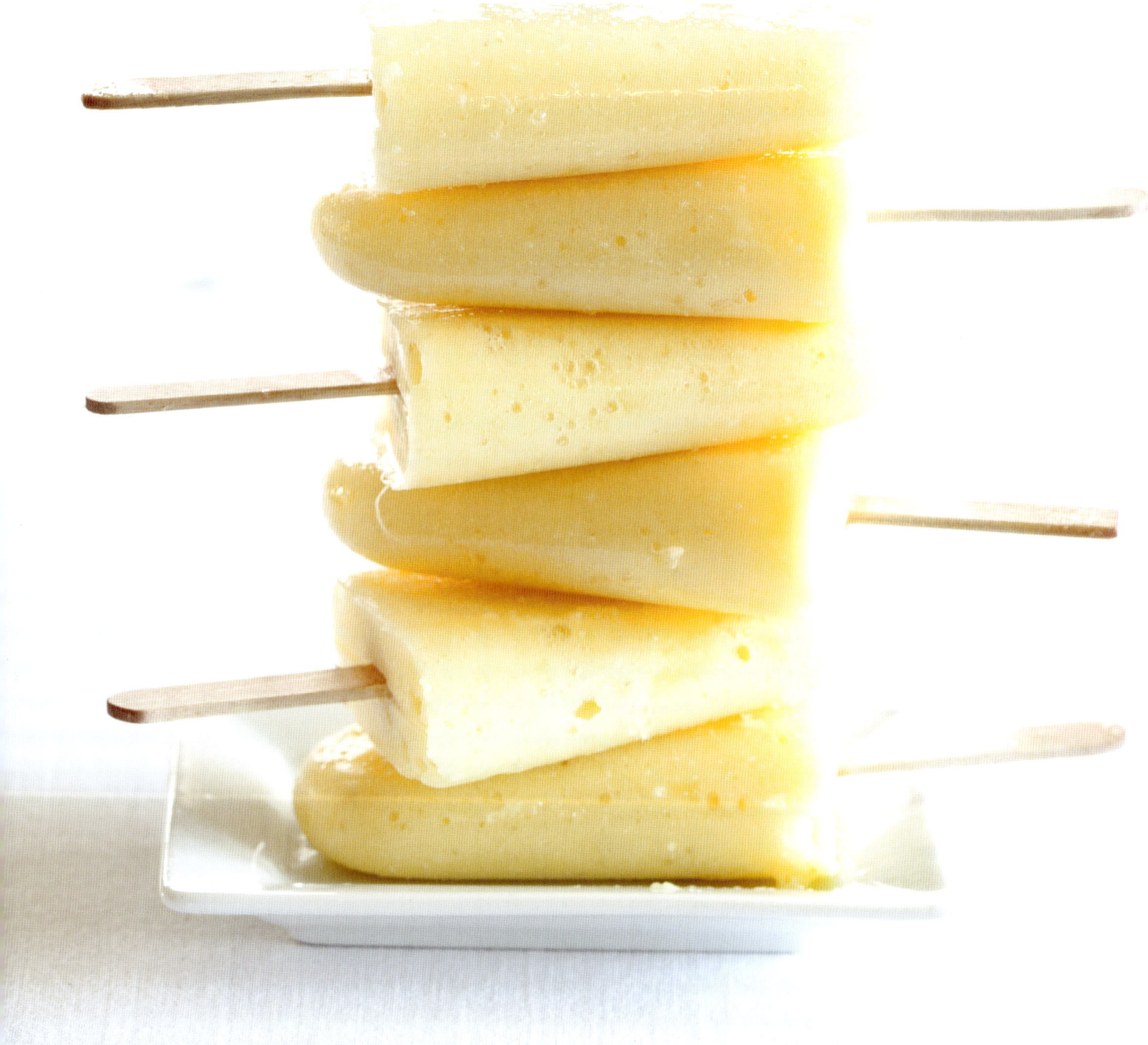

NUTTY CRUNCH SLICE

1 cup sesame seeds
½ cup pumpkin seeds
½ cup sunflower seeds
1 cup desiccated coconut
1 cup chopped almonds
1 x 250 g packet gingernut biscuits
½ cup chopped dried apricots
125 g butter, chopped
½ cup sweetened condensed milk

Grease and line a 20 cm x 30 cm shallow baking tin.

Place the sesame seeds, pumpkin seeds, sunflower seeds, coconut and almonds in a non-stick frying pan. Stir constantly over a low to medium heat for 6–8 minutes, until toasted. Transfer to a bowl.

Place the gingernuts in a food processor and process until they are fine crumbs. Stir the crumbs and apricots into the toasted mixture.

Place the butter and condensed milk in a small saucepan. Stir over a low heat until the butter has melted. Pour over the dry ingredients and mix well.

Press the mixture over the base of the tin. Cover and refrigerate for 1 hour. Cut to desired size and store in the refrigerator.

CRANBERRY MEATLOAF

500 g lean mince
¼ cup cooked rice
¼ cup tomato sauce
½ cup breadcrumbs
1 egg
1 small onion, very finely chopped
1 tsp salt

Topping
1 cup cranberry jelly
1 tbsp brown sugar
1 tsp lemon juice

Preheat oven to 180°C. Line a loaf tin with non-stick baking paper.

In a mixing bowl, place mince, rice, tomato sauce, breadcrumbs, egg, onion and salt.
Mix together until well combined. Press firmly into loaf tin.

For the topping, mix together cranberry jelly, brown sugar and lemon juice.
Spoon over top of loaf and bake for 45 minutes. Slice and serve.

Serves 4–6

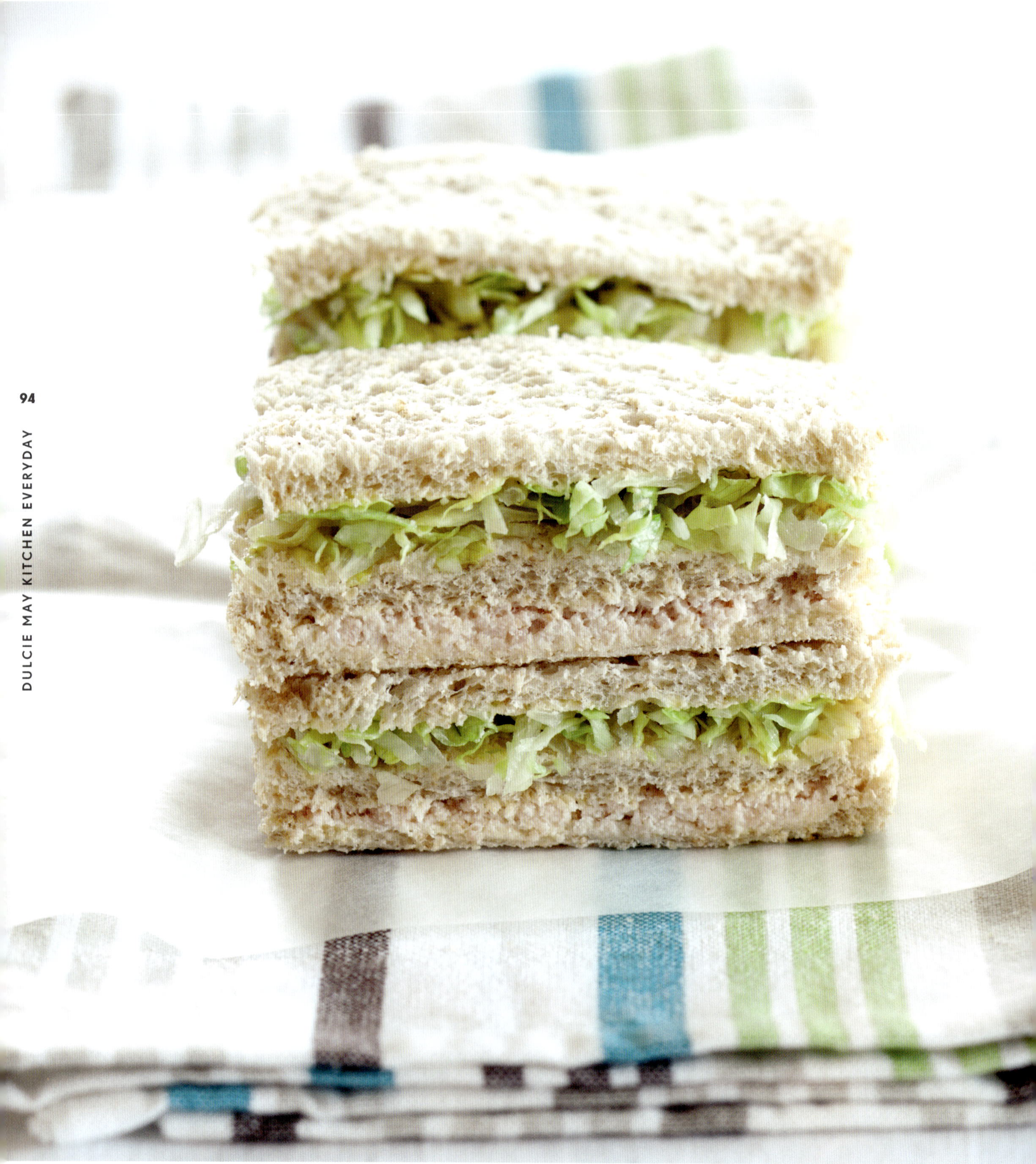

HAM AND CRUNCHY LETTUCE SANDWICHES

400 g ham
100 g cream cheese
50 g butter, softened
1 loaf brown or white bread
2 cups shredded iceberg lettuce

Put the ham and cream cheese in a food processor and mix until a smooth paste forms.

Butter all the bread.

Lay out a third of the bread slices and spread all the ham mixture evenly between the slices.

Lay a second piece of bread on top of the filling, butter-side up. Place shredded lettuce over the bread and top with remaining pieces of bread, butter-side down.

Trim off crusts and cut into desired shape.

Makes 8 whole sandwiches

JELLIED RHUBARB

6–8 stalks rhubarb
4 tbsp water
¼ cup sugar
2 packets strawberry jelly
1 cup pineapple juice
whipped cream
chocolate flake

Chop rhubarb into 2 cm lengths. Put in a pan, add water and sugar and bring to the boil then turn to a low heat. Cook for 10 minutes until tender. Remove from heat. Add jelly crystals and stir gently until jelly is dissolved. Stir in pineapple juice.

Pour into a large bowl or individual serving dishes. Refrigerate until set and serve with whipped cream and pieces of chocolate flake.

Serves 4–6

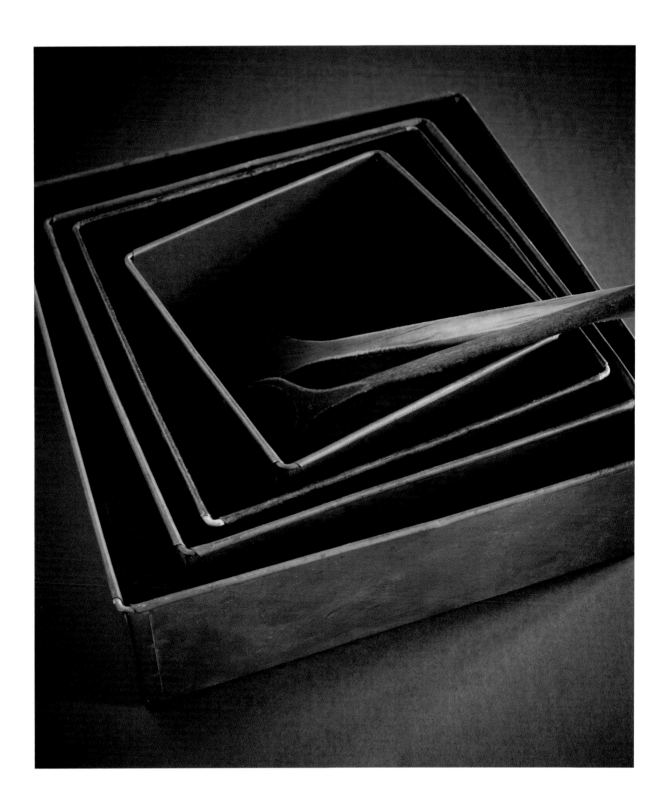

CAKES AND LOAVES

DATE AND GINGER CAKE WITH CARAMEL ICING

250 g pitted dates, finely chopped
1 tsp baking soda
1 cup hot black coffee
2 eggs, lightly beaten
1/3 cup grated fresh ginger
1 tsp vanilla essence
100 g butter
1/3 cup brown sugar
1/2 cup treacle
1 2/3 cups standard flour
1/2 tsp baking powder

1 tsp ground cinnamon
5 dates, pitted and sliced, to decorate
1/2 cup walnuts, chopped, to decorate

Caramel Icing
50 g butter
1/2 cup brown sugar, packed
1/2 cup cream
1/2 tsp vanilla essence
2 cups icing sugar

Preheat oven to 180°C. Line and grease a 22 cm round cake tin.

Place the dates, baking soda and coffee in a bowl and set aside for 20 minutes. Then blend the date mixture to form a paste and tip into a bowl. Stir in eggs, fresh ginger and vanilla.

Cream butter and sugar until light and fluffy, then add treacle, and add sifted flour, baking powder and cinnamon. Fold in date mixture and pour into tin. Bake for 40–45 minutes. Leave to cool in tin.

To make icing, melt butter and brown sugar in a pot, bring to the boil and cook for 1 minute. Remove from heat and stir in the cream and vanilla. Add the sifted icing sugar and mix to make a smooth icing. Allow to cool, stirring occasionally until thick in consistency. Spread icing evenly over cooled cake and decorate with dates and walnuts.

Makes 1 x 22 cm round cake

CARROT CAKE WITH CREAM CHEESE ICING

1 cup wholemeal flour
1 cup standard white flour
2 tsp baking soda
1 tsp ground cinnamon
¼ tsp salt
1 cup bran
2 cups raw sugar
1 cup cooking oil
4 eggs, beaten
3 cups grated carrot
⅓ cup sultanas
⅓ cup chopped walnuts

Cream Cheese Icing
125 g cream cheese
30 g butter, softened
2 cups icing sugar

Preheat oven to 180°C. Line a 25 cm square cake tin with non-stick baking paper.

In a large bowl, sift flours, baking soda, cinnamon and salt. Add bran and raw sugar, mixing to combine. Make a well, stir in oil, beaten egg, carrot, sultanas and walnuts and mix together. Pour into cake tin.

Bake for 1 hour. Allow to cool in tin.

Blend all icing ingredients together in a food processor and spread evenly on cooled cake, or serve on the side.

Makes 1 x 25 cm square cake

UPSIDE-DOWN APPLE CAKE

3 apples, cored and thinly sliced
juice of 1 lemon
50 g butter
1 cup brown sugar
1 egg
1 cup caster sugar
2 cups self-raising flour
250 ml cream
1 tsp vanilla essence

Preheat oven to 180°C.

Combine the apples in a bowl with the lemon juice and set aside.

Place the butter in a 22 cm round cake tin and put in the oven for a few minutes to melt. Remove and sprinkle with brown sugar. Arrange apples on top.

Beat the egg well until light and creamy. Gradually add the caster sugar, beating constantly. Sift the flour into a separate bowl and mix into the creamed mixture alternately with the combined cream and vanilla essence.

Spoon mixture over the apples and place in the oven for 40–45 minutes.

Cool for 10 minutes in the tin and then turn out on cake rack to cool completely.

Makes 1 x 22 cm round cake

BLUEBERRY AND LEMON LOAF

125 g butter
¾ cup caster sugar
zest of 1 lemon, finely grated
2 eggs
1½ cups self-raising flour, sifted
½ cup freshly squeezed lemon juice
1 cup blueberries

Lemon Icing
100 g icing sugar
1 tsp butter, melted
1 tbsp lemon juice, strained

Preheat oven to 180°C. Grease and line a 23 cm loaf tin.

Cream butter and sugar, add zest and beat in eggs, one at a time. Stir in flour and lemon juice and fold until combined. Gently fold in blueberries.

Spoon mixture into tin and bake for 45–50 minutes or until cooked through.

Cool loaf in tin for 10 minutes and then remove to a wire rack to cool completely.

Combine icing sugar, butter and lemon juice to make icing. Stir until smooth and runny, then spread over the cold loaf.

Makes 1 x 23 cm loaf

CARROT AND GINGER LOAF WITH CINNAMON FROSTING

100 g butter
½ cup brown sugar
2 tbsp treacle
2 tbsp golden syrup
3 cups grated carrot
2 eggs, beaten
1⅓ cups self-raising flour
¼ tsp baking soda
4 tsp ground ginger

Cinnamon Frosting
75 g cream cheese
1 cup icing sugar
1 tsp cinnamon

Preheat oven to 180°C. Grease and line a 23 cm loaf tin.

In a pot, place butter, sugar, treacle and golden syrup. Gently heat until everything is melted together.

Add carrot, eggs and sifted flour, baking soda and ginger. Mix until well combined. Pour into tin and bake for 35–40 minutes.

Cool in tin for 10 minutes. Remove and place on wire rack to cool completely.

Blend all frosting ingredients together in a food processor, then spread evenly over loaf.

Makes 1 x 23 cm loaf

DRIED APRICOT LOAF

1 cup sugar
½ cup chopped dried apricots
½ cup chopped dates
½ cup sultanas
½ cup currants
50 g butter, melted
1 tsp vanilla essence
½ tsp salt
1 cup boiling water
1 egg
2 cups self-raising flour

Preheat oven to 180°C. Grease and line a 23 cm loaf tin.

Place sugar, dried fruit, butter, vanilla and salt in a bowl and pour over boiling water. Leave to cool.

When cool, mix in egg and sifted flour. Fold to combine.

Place mixture in loaf tin. Bake for 40–45 minutes.

Makes 1 x 23 cm loaf

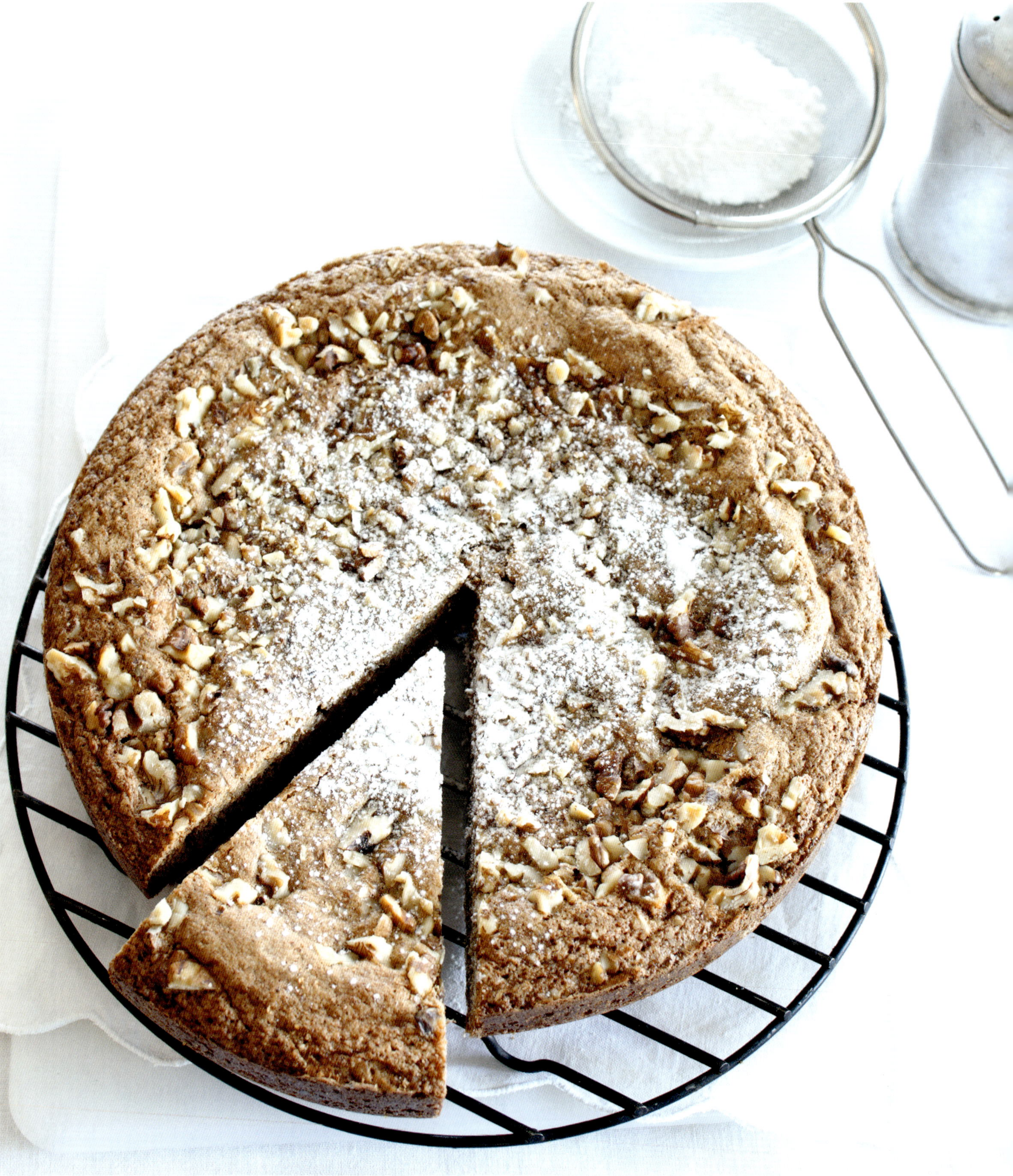

NUTMEG CAKE

1½ cups wholemeal flour
1½ cups brown sugar
150 g butter
2 eggs, lightly beaten
2 tsp baking powder
2 whole nutmegs, grated
½ cup chopped walnuts
icing sugar, for dusting
cream, to serve

Preheat oven to 180°C. Grease and line a 20 to 25 cm spring-form cake tin.

In a bowl, mix the flour and sugar together. Rub in the butter to resemble breadcrumbs.

Put half the flour, sugar and butter mixture in the cake tin.

Mix the egg, baking powder and nutmeg into the other half of the mixture. Pour over the bottom layer. Sprinkle with walnuts. Bake for 30 minutes.

Dust with icing sugar and serve warm with cream.

Makes 1 x 20 to 25 cm round cake

LEMON AND PASSION FRUIT LOAF

4 eggs
1¼ cups caster sugar
¼ tsp salt
1⅔ cups standard flour
½ tsp baking powder
zest of 4 lemons, finely grated
½ cup passion fruit yoghurt
100 g butter, melted and cooled

Passion Fruit Icing
100 g icing sugar
1 tsp butter, melted
1 tbsp passion fruit pulp

Preheat oven to 180°C. Lightly grease a large loaf tin with oil spray and line with baking paper.

Beat eggs in an electric mixer for 1 minute. Add sugar and salt and continue to beat until thick and creamy. Fold in sifted flour and baking powder, then add lemon zest, yoghurt and melted butter and mix to combine.

Pour into loaf tin and bake for 45 minutes. Cool in tin for 10 minutes, then remove and place on wire rack to cool completely.

Combine icing sugar, butter and passion fruit pulp to make the icing. Stir until smooth and runny, then spread over cold loaf.

Makes 1 large loaf

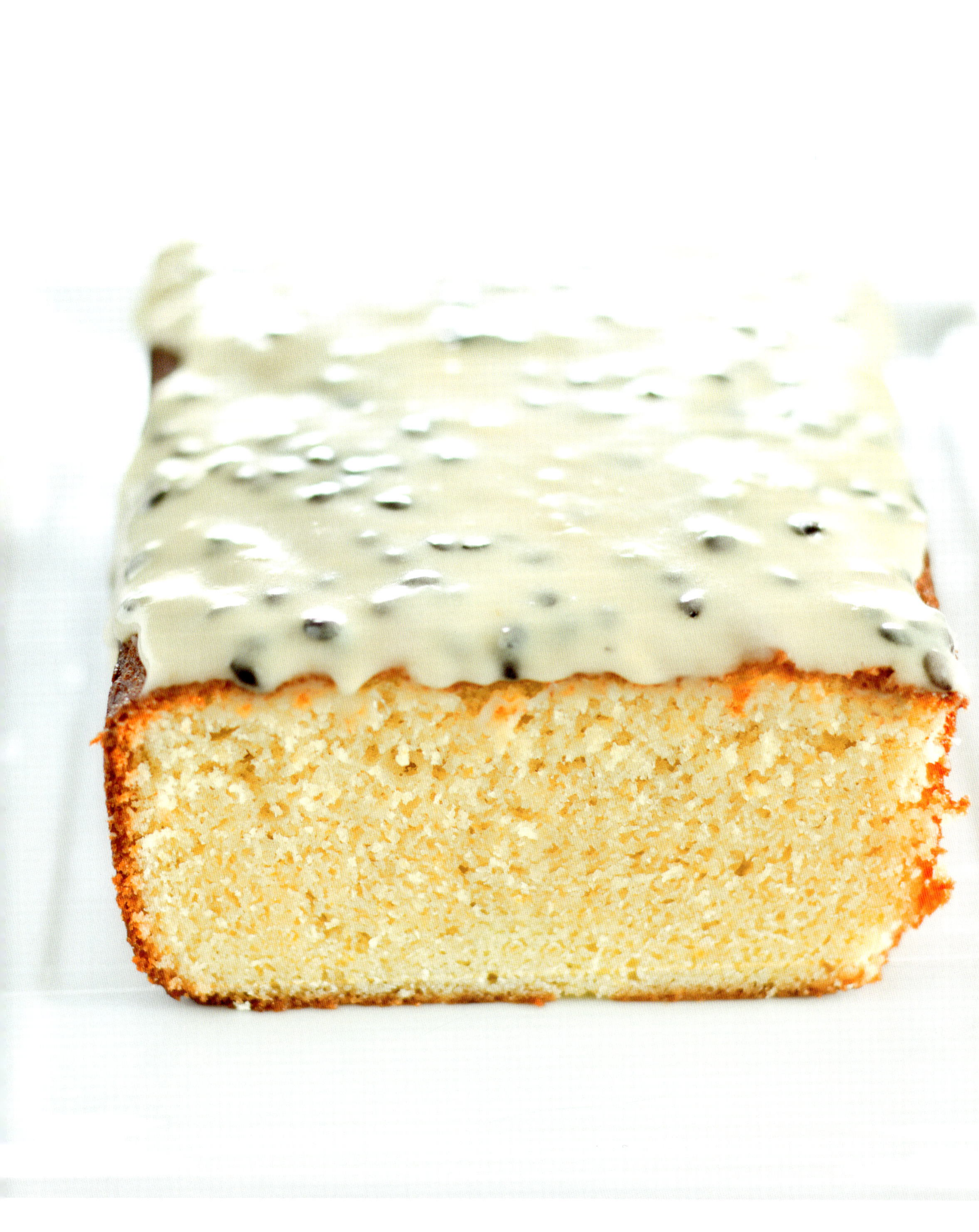

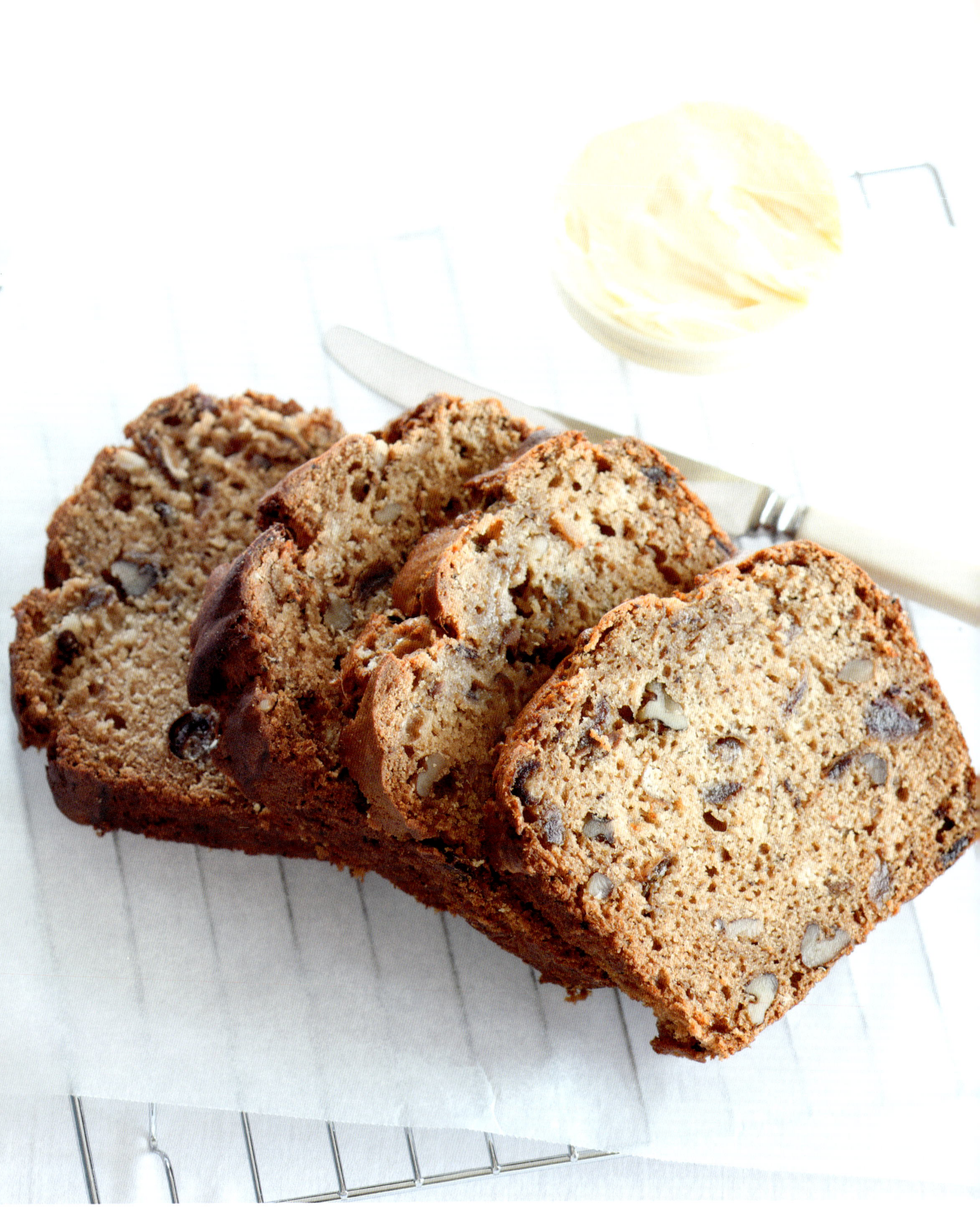

DATE AND WALNUT LOAF

1½ cups boiling water
1½ cups chopped dates
½ cup oil
1 cup brown sugar
1 egg
1 tsp vanilla essence
1½ cups standard flour
1 tsp baking soda
1 tsp baking powder
½ tsp salt
½ cup chopped walnuts

Preheat oven to 180°C. Line a 23 cm loaf tin with non-stick baking paper.

Pour boiling water over the dates. Add the oil and cool.

Add sugar, egg and vanilla essence and beat lightly. Sift in the flour, baking soda, baking powder and salt. Mix until just moist. Add the walnuts and fold through.

Pour into loaf tin and bake for 1 hour.

Makes 1 x 23 cm loaf

NEAPOLITAN CAKE

250 g butter, softened
1¼ cups caster sugar
1 tsp vanilla essence
3 eggs
2¼ cups self-raising flour, sifted
¾ cup milk
2 tbsp cocoa powder, sifted
1 tsp raspberry essence

Vanilla Butter Icing
50 g butter, softened
1 cup icing sugar, sifted
1 tsp vanilla essence
2 tbsp boiling water

Preheat oven to 160°C. Grease and line a 23 cm cake tin.

Cream the butter and sugar until light and fluffy. Add vanilla essence and eggs, one at a time. Stir in sifted flour alternately with the milk.

Divide the mixture between three separate bowls. Fold cocoa powder into one portion, raspberry essence into one portion and leave one portion plain.

Drop large spoonfuls of the mixtures into the prepared cake tin, alternating the different colours. Bake for 1 hour, then leave to cool in tin.

Beat all icing ingredients together in a bowl until pale and creamy. Remove cold cake from tin and spread with icing.

Makes 1 x 23 cm cake

DINNER

CRISPY CHICKEN

2 tbsp butter
2 tbsp oil
12 chicken drumsticks
2 tbsp flour
1 tsp salt
1 tsp paprika
1 tsp caster sugar
1 cup sour cream
2 tsp chopped chives

Preheat oven to 200°C.

Put butter and oil in a casserole dish and place in the oven for a few minutes until butter melts. Remove from oven and turn the chicken pieces in the butter to coat completely.

Mix dry ingredients together and use a wire sieve to sprinkle evenly over chicken, turning to ensure coverage.

Bake for 20 minutes then turn and bake for a further 20 minutes.

Serve with sour cream and chives.

Serves 4–6

DUCK WITH OVEN-ROASTED VEGETABLES

6 duck legs

2 tbsp cooking oil

2 onions, peeled and chopped

2 carrots, peeled and chopped

2 parsnips, peeled and chopped

2 whole heads garlic

8 sprigs fresh thyme

4 cups water

2 tbsp Worcestershire sauce

2 tbsp vinegar

pinch of baking soda

2 tsp salt

6 tbsp flour

4 tbsp tomato sauce

1 tsp mustard powder

1 tbsp sugar

Preheat oven to 150°C.

Remove any excess fat from duck legs. Heat oil over medium heat in a large frying pan. Brown duck legs skin-side down for 10–15 minutes or until skin is very golden. Turn over and cook for the same amount of time.

In a large roasting pan, place onion, carrot, parsnip, garlic and thyme. Place duck legs on top of vegetables.

In a separate bowl, whisk together the rest of the ingredients. Pour mixture over vegetables and duck and cover with baking paper. Place lid on top of roasting pan. Cook for 1 hour.

Remove baking paper and lid and cook for a further 30 minutes. Serve with your favourite greens.

Serves 4–6

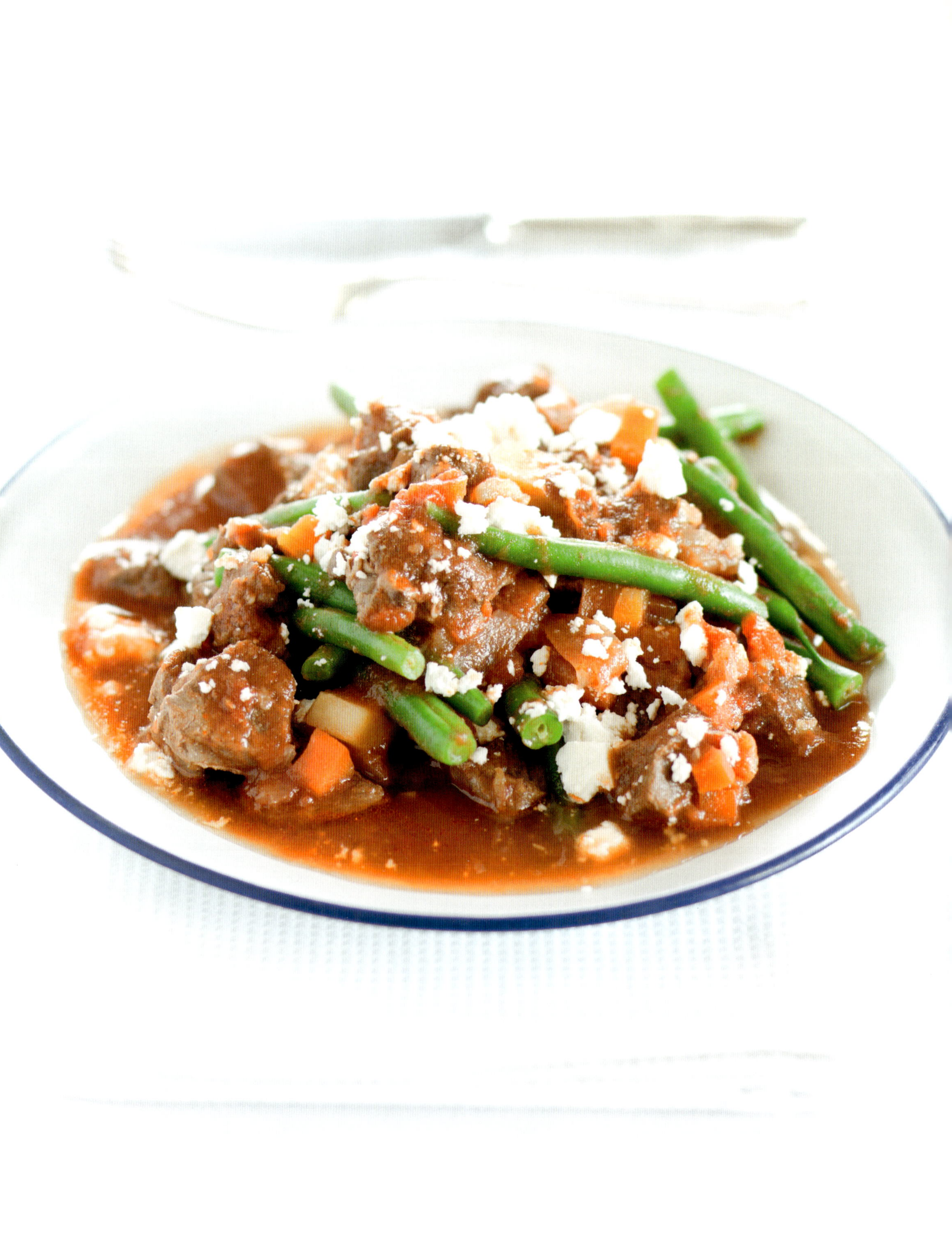

LAMB AND GREEN BEAN CASSEROLE WITH FETA

1 tbsp olive oil
1 kg lamb, diced
2 potatoes, chopped
2 carrots, chopped
2 onions, chopped
2 cloves garlic, chopped
1 bunch fresh thyme
125 ml red wine
1 x 230 g tin chopped tomatoes
1 x 290 g tub tomato paste
250 ml vegetable stock
1 tbsp salt
500 g green beans
200 g feta

In a large saucepan, heat oil and fry the lamb, making sure it is browned on all sides. Add the potato, carrot, onion, garlic and thyme and fry for about 10 minutes. Add wine and let it reduce for a few minutes. Add tomatoes and tomato paste, stir and then add stock. Season with salt. Put a lid on the saucepan and leave to simmer for about 40 minutes or until tender.

Add beans and cook for a further 10 minutes. Once ready to serve, sprinkle with feta.

Serves 4–6

PRAWN AND MINT SALAD

200 g dried vermicelli rice noodles
450 g cooked prawns, peeled
1 large carrot, thinly sliced
¼ small cabbage, shredded
1 large handful mint leaves
⅓ cup cashews, lightly toasted and chopped
2 spring onions, thinly sliced

Dressing
1 red chilli, seeded and chopped
1 clove garlic, crushed
1 tsp ginger, finely grated
¼ cup caster sugar
¼ cup rice vinegar
2 tbsp lime juice

Cook rice noodles according to directions on packet. Once cooked place in a large bowl and add all other ingredients. Toss to combine.

Place all dressing ingredients in a large glass jar and shake to combine. Pour over salad and serve.

Serves 4–6

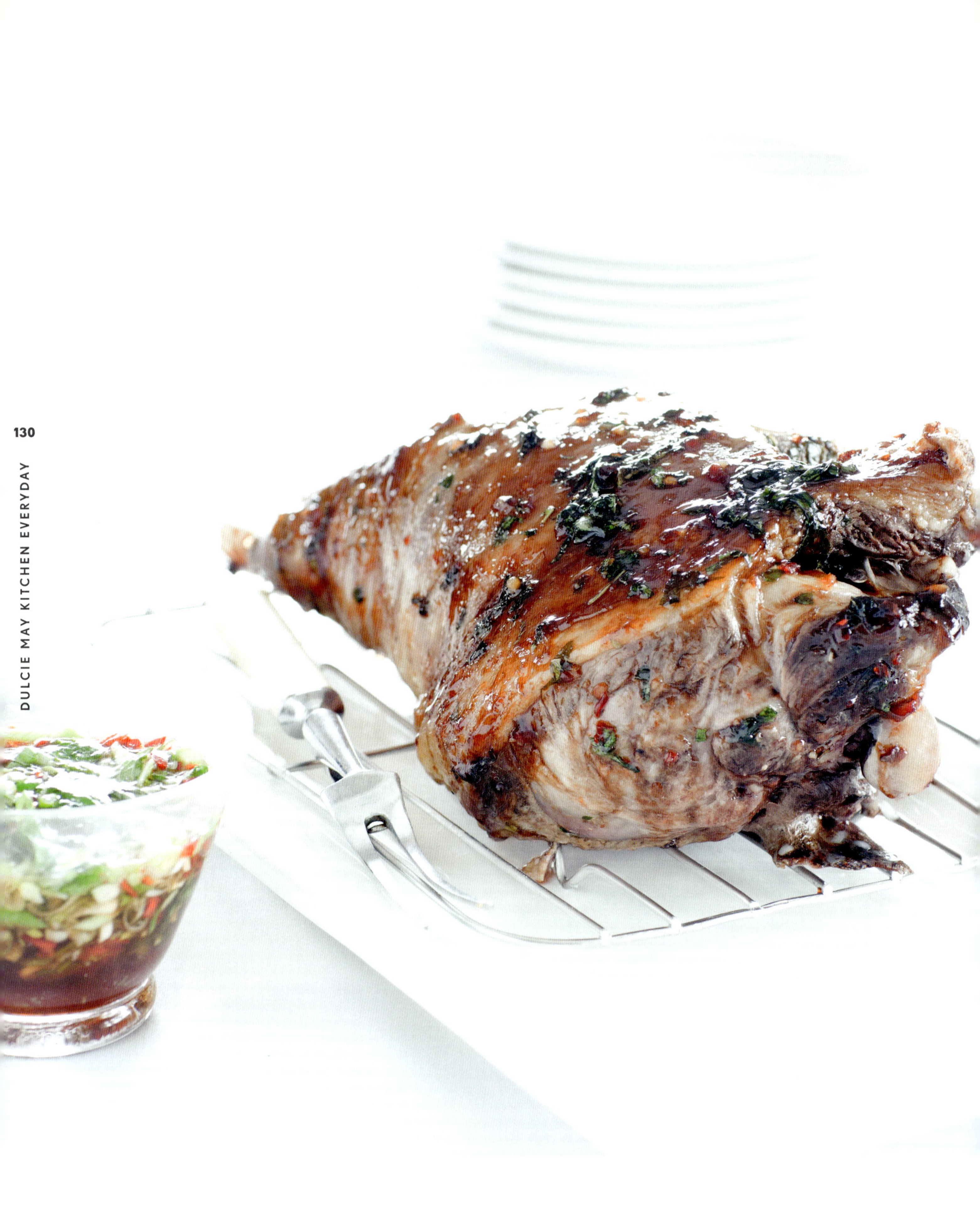

ROAST LAMB WITH THAI-STYLE MINT SAUCE

2½ kg leg of lamb
salt and pepper

Thai-Style Mint Sauce
2 tbsp brown sugar
2 tbsp peanut oil
¼ cup rice vinegar
zest and juice of 1 lime
1 tbsp soy sauce
2 red chillies, seeded and thinly diced
2 spring onions, finely chopped
2 cups mint leaves, roughly chopped

Preheat oven to 180°C.

Place lamb in roasting pan and season with salt and pepper.

Cover loosely with foil. Roast for 1¼ hours, remove foil and roast for a further 30 minutes or until cooked to your liking. Rest for 20–30 minutes loosely covered with foil.

Combine all sauce ingredients in a bowl and mix well. Spoon over lamb before serving.

Serves 8–10

ROAST BEEF WITH RED WINE SAUCE AND VEGETABLES

1.5 kg topside beef
olive oil
salt and pepper
sprigs fresh rosemary

Red Wine Sauce
3 tbsp olive oil
3 onions, finely diced
1 tsp white and black peppercorns, crushed
2 cloves garlic, finely chopped
300 ml red wine
700 ml strong beef stock
2 sprigs fresh thyme
2 sprigs fresh rosemary

Preheat oven to 250°C.

Place beef in a roasting tray and season with olive oil, salt and pepper and rosemary. Turn oven down to 200°C. Cook for 1 hour. Remove from oven and allow to rest for 10 minutes.

Heat oil for sauce in a large saucepan over high heat. Add the onion and cook for 5 minutes or until cooked through. Add the peppercorns and garlic and cook for a further 2 minutes. Add the wine and simmer until almost dry. Add the stock and bring to the boil, then reduce the heat and simmer for 20 minutes or until reduced by half.

Strain through a fine sieve into a small saucepan and bring back to a simmer for 10 minutes or until it thickens.

Remove from heat and add the herbs. Cover and set aside for 10 minutes. Pass through a fine sieve to remove the herbs and keep the sauce warm until needed.

Serve with vegetables prepared as on page 134.

Vegetables

¼ cup olive oil
1½ cups vegetable stock
1 clove garlic, thinly sliced
3 sprigs fresh thyme
2 tsp sea salt
20 pickling onions, peeled
16 baby carrots, tops trimmed and peeled
½ small cauliflower, cut into florets
12 button mushrooms, steamed
1 large vine tomato, diced
2 tbsp chopped flat-leaf parsley

In a large pot, combine the oil, stock, garlic, thyme and salt. Bring to the boil. Add the onions and simmer for 20 minutes. Then add the carrots, cauliflower and button mushrooms and simmer for another 5 minutes.

Drain vegetables and place in a large, shallow serving dish along with the tomato and fresh parsley. Toss to combine.

Serves 8–10

BEEF CURRY WITH TURMERIC RICE

2 tbsp cooking oil
500 g gravy beef, cubed
2 cloves garlic, crushed
2 onions, diced
1 large apple, peeled, cored and sliced
2 tbsp curry powder
25 g flour
600 ml beef stock
1 x 165 ml tin coconut milk
4 tomatoes, chopped
1 tbsp tomato chutney
50 g sultanas
juice of 1 lemon
salt and pepper

Heat oil in a frying pan over medium heat and add meat to brown. Transfer to a large pot. In the pan, gently fry garlic, onions and apple until soft and add to meat. Wipe the pan dry and dry-fry curry powder and flour for 2–3 minutes. Gradually add stock, stirring continuously, then add coconut milk, tomatoes, tomato chutney, sultanas and lemon juice and season with salt and pepper.

Pour sauce over meat and simmer until cooked, approximately 2 hours.

Serve with turmeric rice (see page 136).

Turmeric Rice

450 g basmati rice
3 tbsp oil
1 cinnamon stick
3 cloves
½ tsp turmeric powder
1 tsp salt
650 ml water

Wash the rice under cold water until water runs clear.

Heat oil in a pot over medium heat and add cinnamon stick and cloves. Fry for 30–40 seconds. Add rice, turmeric and salt and gently stir for 1 minute. Add water and bring to the boil. Cover and reduce to a very low heat and cook for 20 minutes. Separate with fork. Serve with beef curry (previous page).

Serves 10–12

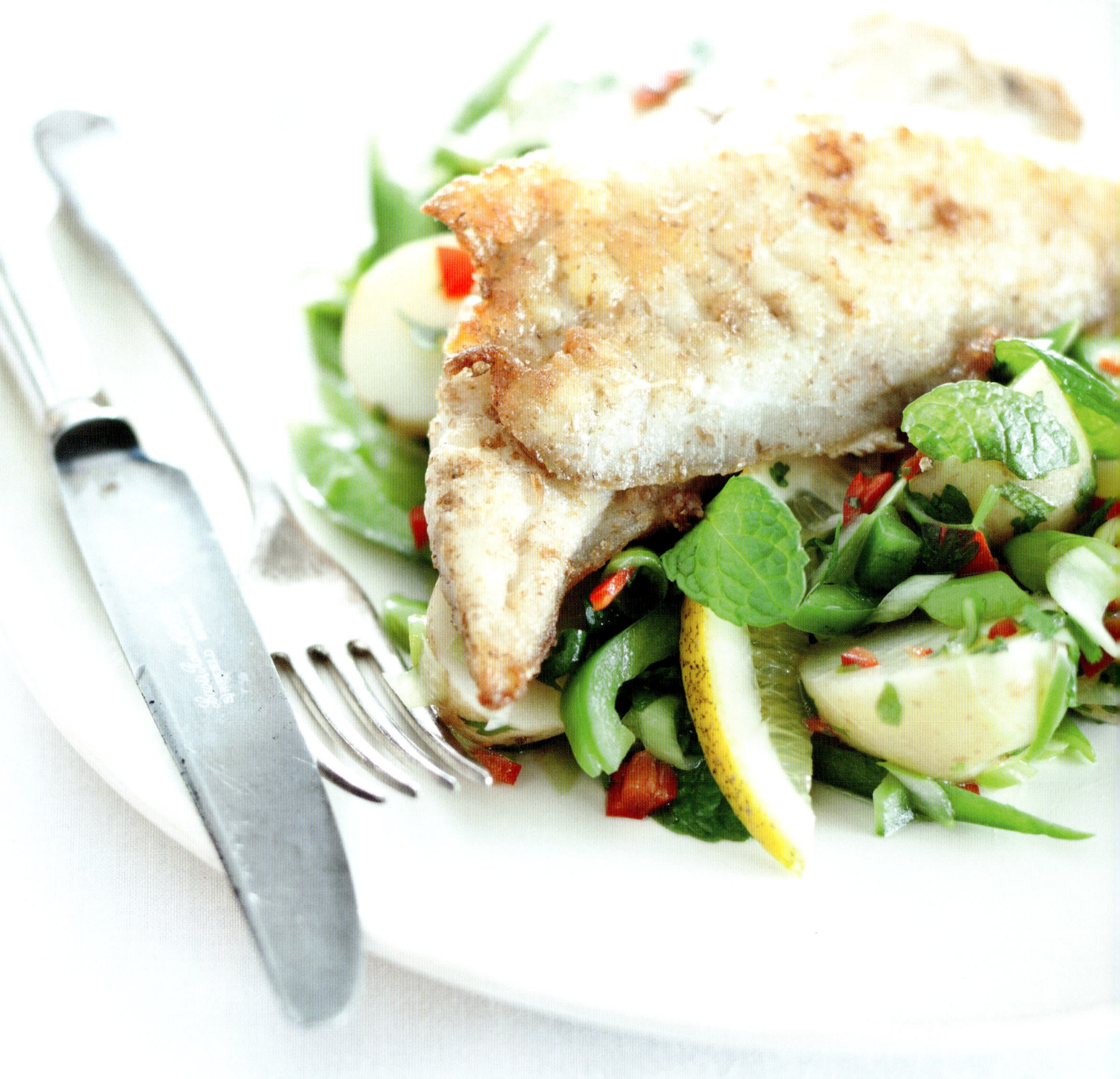

PAN-FRIED SNAPPER WITH POTATO, LEMON AND HERB SALAD

400 g potatoes
½ tsp salt
¼ cup olive oil
juice of ½ lemon
salt and pepper
1 small green capsicum, diced

2 large red chillies, seeded and diced
¼ cup chopped mint
½ cup chopped flat-leaf parsley
6 spring onions, finely sliced
1 tbsp olive oil
4 fillets fresh snapper, skin removed

Bring a large pot of water to the boil. Add potatoes and salt and simmer for 8–10 minutes. Drain.

Place the olive oil and lemon juice in a bowl and stir to combine. Season with salt and pepper.

Pour half the dressing over the hot potatoes cut into chunks. To the remaining dressing add the capsicum, chilli, mint, parsley and spring onion and mix gently. Leave potatoes to cool before combining with salad.

Heat a little oil in large frying pan until hot. Add the fish and cook for 3 minutes. Turn and cook on the other side for 2–3 minutes or until the fish is just cooked. Serve fish with potato, lemon and herb salad.

Serves 4

ROAST CAPSICUM FILLED WITH RISOTTO AND FRESH HERBS

2 tbsp olive oil
20 g butter
1 large brown onion, finely chopped
1½ cups arborio rice
3⅓ cups vegetable stock
½ cup finely grated Parmesan

½ cup pine nuts, toasted
½ cup roughly chopped flat-leaf parsley
½ cup roughly chopped basil leaves
6 red or yellow capsicums
¼ cup olive oil, extra

Preheat oven to 180°C. Line a roasting pan with non-stick baking paper.

Heat oil and butter in a large ovenproof saucepan. Add onion and cook for 5 minutes or until soft. Add rice and cook for 1 minute. Add vegetable stock, stirring to combine. Bring to the boil and cover. Place in the oven and cook for 20 minutes.

Remove from oven and add Parmesan and pine nuts, mixing until cheese has melted. Cool. Once cooled add fresh herbs.

Cut tops off capsicums and scoop out seeds to remove. Fill capsicums with risotto mix and place lids back on top. Place in roasting pan and drizzle with olive oil. Place in the oven and cook for 30 minutes or until capsicums are soft.

Serves 6

COURGETTE, LEEK AND RICOTTA LASAGNE WITH FRESH HERBS

3 tbsp olive oil
3 cloves garlic, crushed
3 leeks, thinly sliced
6 courgettes, roughly sliced
2 x 400 g tins crushed tomatoes
1 x 420 g tin tomato soup
½ cup chopped parsley
½ cup chopped basil

salt and pepper
450 g ricotta
4 eggs
50 g butter
2 tbsp standard flour
1½ cups milk
400 g fresh lasagne sheets

Preheat oven to 180°C. Grease a large lasagne dish.

Heat oil in large pan, add garlic and leek and cook for 8–10 minutes or until soft but not brown. Add courgette, tomatoes and tomato soup. Bring to the boil and simmer for 8–10 minutes. Add parsley and basil and season with salt and pepper. Set aside to cool.

In a separate bowl, mix together ricotta and eggs until well combined.

For the white sauce, heat the butter in a pot over medium heat. Once melted add flour and cook for 1 minute. Slowly add milk, stirring constantly until combined. Reduce heat and simmer for 1 minute.

Place one sheet of fresh lasagne at bottom of dish. Place half of the tomato mix on top followed by half of the ricotta mix and repeat process starting with lasagne sheet. Place last lasagne sheet on top of ricotta mix and pour over white sauce.

Cook for 30–40 minutes or until bubbling and golden.

Serves 4–6

PUDDINGS

MINT AND CHOCOLATE CHIP ICE CREAM

400 g mascarpone
4 eggs, separated
1 tsp mint essence
1 tsp green food colouring
100 g caster sugar
200 g chocolate chips

In a large bowl, beat the mascarpone with the egg yolks, mint essence and food colouring until well combined.

In a separate bowl, whisk the egg whites until stiff. Then gradually beat in the sugar, a little at a time, until thick and glossy. Fold this into the mascarpone mixture.

Transfer to a bowl and place in the freezer. Beat every 30 minutes for a few hours. Lastly add in chocolate chips.

Spoon into tub then freeze overnight to set completely.

Serves 4–6

HONEY AND WHISKY ICE CREAM

4 egg yolks
4 tbsp liquid honey
4 tbsp whisky
300 ml cream, whipped

In a bowl, beat egg yolks until pale. Heat honey in a small pot until at boiling point. Gradually add honey to eggs until all combined and beat for 10 minutes.

Add whisky and whipped cream.

Pour mixture into tray or bowl and freeze.

Serves 4–6

APPLE FRITTERS

1 cup standard flour
½ tsp salt
1 egg, lightly beaten
⅔ cup milk
4 cooking apples, cored and peeled
oil, for deep-frying
½ cup caster sugar
½ tsp ground cinnamon
125 g mascarpone

Sift flour and salt into a bowl. Make a well in the centre and add egg and milk.
Beat until blended and smooth. Leave to stand for 1 hour.

Cut apples into rings. Coat rings with batter and carefully add a few at a time to
a pan of very hot oil. Cook, turning often, until golden brown. Drain on paper towels
and repeat process until all apples have been cooked.

Mix together the caster sugar and cinnamon in a small bowl.

Serve the fritters with the cinnamon sugar and mascarpone.

Makes 16

CHOCOLATE SAUCE

100 g butter
¾ cup cocoa
2 tsp vanilla essence
8 tbsp water
½ cup sugar
1 tbsp golden syrup

Place all ingredients in a small saucepan. Stir until melted and well combined.
Serve warm with dessert.

Makes 1½ cups

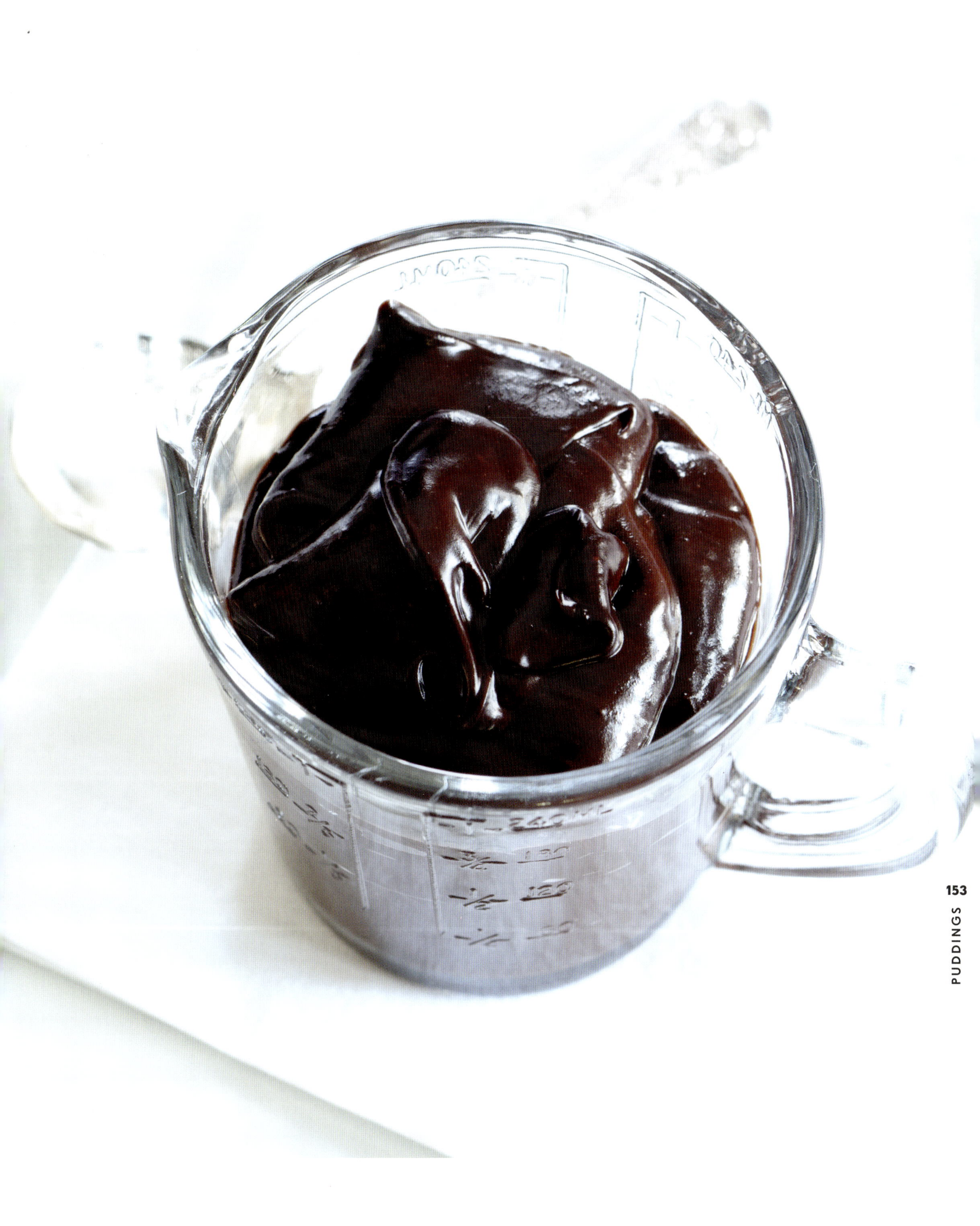

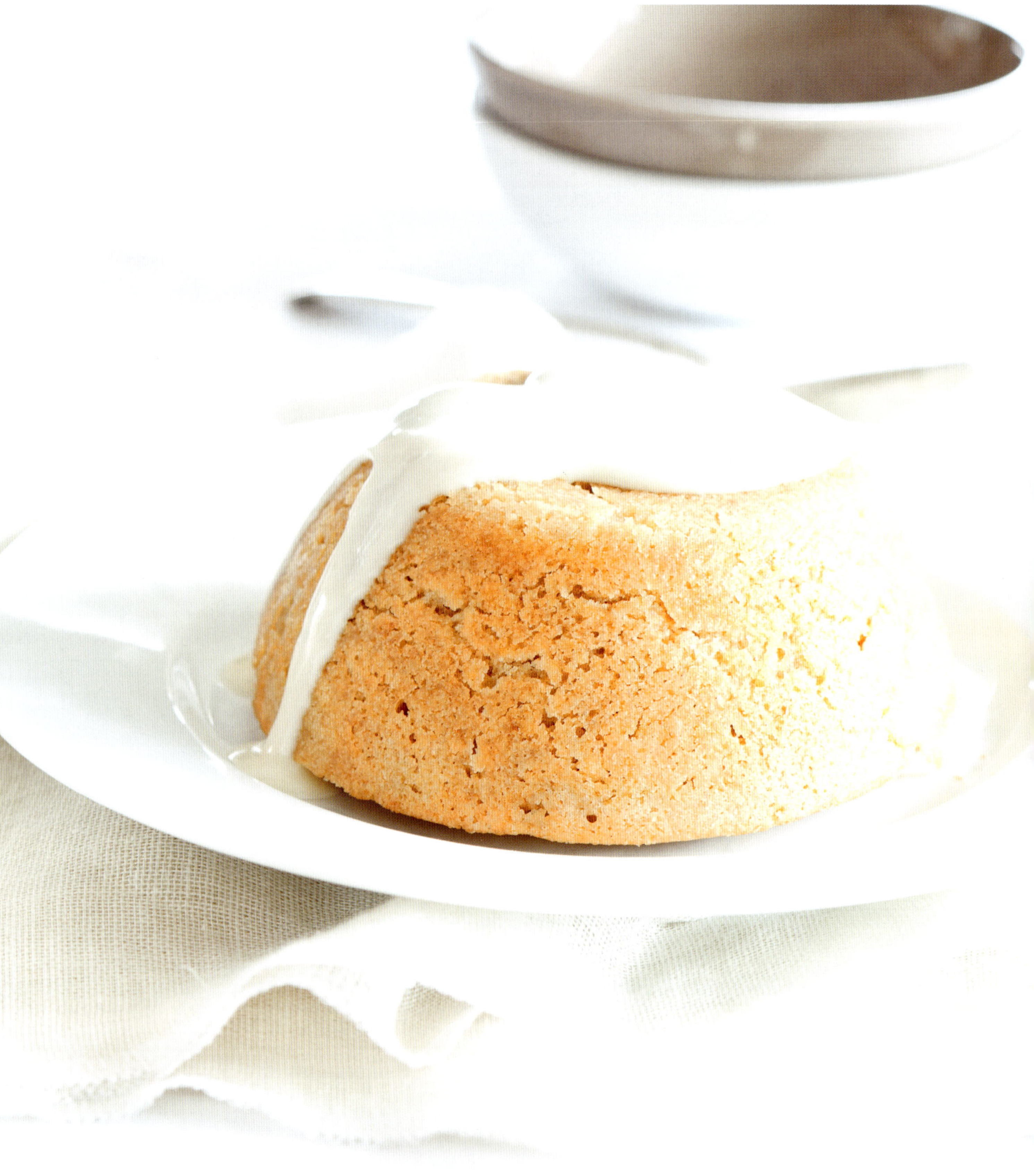

GINGER STEAMED PUDDING WITH BRANDY SAUCE

100 g butter
½ cup sugar
2 eggs
1 tbsp grated fresh ginger
½ tsp vanilla essence
1 cup self-raising flour
2 tbsp ground ginger
½ cup milk

Brandy Sauce
40 g butter
30 g standard flour
250 ml milk
2 tbsp caster sugar
2 tbsp brandy

Grease a steamed-pudding bowl with butter. Half-fill a large saucepan with water and bring to the boil. Place a saucer or egg ring in the bottom of the pan for resting the pudding bowl on.

Cream the butter and sugar until light and fluffy. Add the eggs, one at a time, and beat well. Add fresh ginger and vanilla essence.

Sift the flour and ground ginger into a separate bowl. Add alternately with the milk to the creamed mixture, folding gently to combine.

Spoon the mixture into the steamed-pudding bowl. Secure the lid and carefully place in the boiling water, making sure the water comes halfway up the sides of the bowl. Cover the saucepan with a lid and simmer gently for 1 hour.

In a pot, melt butter for sauce, add flour and milk and start whisking until sauce becomes thick. Add the sugar, turn down the heat and allow to gently simmer for 10 minutes, stirring occasionally with a wooden spoon. Turn off heat and stir in brandy. Serve with warm pudding.

Serves 4–6

PASSION FRUIT AND WHITE CHOCOLATE CHEESECAKE

250 g round wine biscuits, crushed
100 g butter, melted
500 g cream cheese, softened
¼ cup caster sugar
⅔ cup cream
2 tsp gelatine dissolved in ¼ cup boiling water
200 g white chocolate, melted
2 tbsp passion fruit pulp

Thoroughly grease a 20 cm spring-form cake tin and line the base with non-stick baking paper.

Combine the biscuit crumbs with the melted butter and press into cake tin. Refrigerate for 15 minutes.

In a large mixing bowl, combine the cream cheese, sugar, cream and gelatine and beat with an electric beater. Add melted chocolate and passion fruit pulp and mix well. Pour the mixture into the prepared tin.

Refrigerate for about 3 hours or until set.

Makes 1 x 20 cm cake

PLUM PUDDING

1 x 850 g tin Black Doris plums, drained and pitted
2 tbsp standard flour
½ tsp salt
5 tbsp sugar
4 eggs
600 ml milk
2 tsp lemon zest
icing sugar, for dusting

Preheat oven to 180°C. Grease a shallow, 6-cup capacity baking dish.

Place plums in baking dish.

In a separate bowl, sift the flour, salt and sugar. Make a well in the centre and add the eggs, one at a time, mixing well after each addition. Gradually add milk, a little at a time, until all combined. Lastly, mix in lemon zest. Pour mixture over the plums through a strainer.

Bake for 45 minutes. Remove from oven and dust with icing sugar. Serve immediately.

Serves 4–6

RICH CHOCOLATE MOUSSE

300 g dark chocolate, chopped
300 ml cream
1 tbsp rum
4 egg whites
¼ cup caster sugar
½ cup cream, extra

Place chocolate in a food processor and process until finely grated.

In a large saucepan, heat cream to just below boiling point. Gradually add cream to chocolate while food processor is still operating. Then add rum and mix until smooth. Transfer chocolate mixture to a large bowl.

Beat egg whites in a small bowl with electric mixer until soft peaks form. Gradually add sugar, a tablespoon at a time, beating well after each addition.

Fold egg white mixture through chocolate mixture.

Whip extra cream until soft peaks form and fold through chocolate mixture. Pour mixture into 8 serving glasses. Refrigerate overnight.

Serves 8

COFFEE CREAM PIE

250 g wine biscuits
½ tsp cinnamon
180 g butter, melted
1 tbsp gelatine
½ cup cold water
½ cup hot water
2 tbsp instant coffee
2 eggs, separated
¾ cup sugar
175 g cream cheese
300 ml cream, whipped

Crush biscuits finely and with cinnamon. Add melted butter and press over base and sides of 23 cm loose-bottomed tin. Chill.

In a saucepan, soften gelatine in cold water. Add hot water and instant coffee and stir over low heat until gelatine has dissolved.

In a separate bowl, beat together egg yolks and ½ cup sugar until light and fluffy. Add to slightly cooled coffee and gelatine mixture, mix well and refrigerate until the consistency of unbeaten egg whites.

Beat the cream cheese with remaining sugar until soft. Gradually add coffee mixture until all combined. Fold in stiffly beaten egg whites and whipped cream. Pour into crumb crust and refrigerate until set.

Serves 10–12

STRAWBERRY MERINGUES

4 egg whites, at room temperature
1½ cups caster sugar
1 tbsp cornflour
1 tsp white vinegar
1 tsp strawberry essence
whipped cream
1 cup fresh strawberries

Preheat oven to 180°C. Line a baking tray with non-stick paper.

Place the egg whites in a large bowl and beat until soft peaks form. Gradually add the sugar, beating constantly. Continue beating until thick and glossy.

In a separate bowl, mix together cornflour, vinegar and strawberry essence. Add to the egg white mixture and beat for a further 5 minutes.

Divide the mixture into six even portions and place on baking tray, keeping the portions as round as possible.

Turn oven down to 100°C. Place tray in oven and cook for 45 minutes. Turn off oven and open the door slightly and leave meringues to cool.

Once cooled place on serving platter and decorate with whipped cream and fresh strawberries.

Serves 6

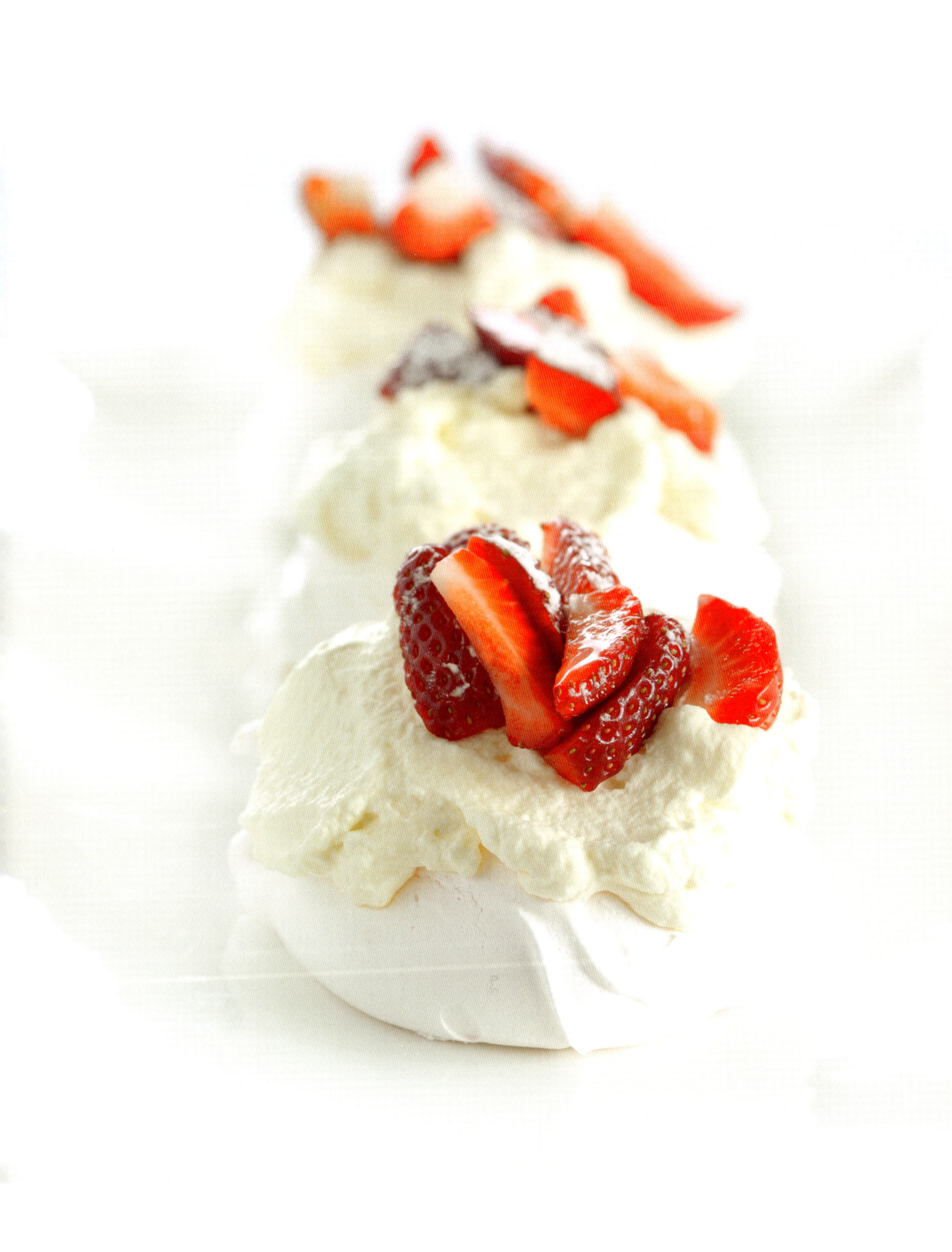

LEMON MERINGUE BAKED ALASKAS

200 g piece of sponge
4 scoops passion fruit ice cream
1 cup lemon curd
4 egg whites
¾ cup sugar

Cut sponge to fit bases of 4 round moulds or small soufflé dishes. Place a scoop of ice cream on top of sponge then pour over lemon curd and cover with more sponge. Place in freezer overnight.

Preheat oven to 200°C.

With an electric beater, beat the egg whites until stiff. Pour in sugar and beat until smooth and glossy.

Use a knife to loosen the sponges from the moulds and place them on a baking tray. Cover each sponge with meringue and bake for 6–8 minutes until meringue has set and is starting to lightly brown. Serve immediately.

Serves 4

BAKED CHEESECAKE

100 g round wine biscuits, crushed
60 g butter, melted
2 tbsp cornflour
2 tbsp water
500 g cream cheese
250 g fresh ricotta
4 eggs
1 cup caster sugar
1 tsp vanilla essence
1 punnet strawberries, hulled

Preheat oven to 150°C. Grease a 20 cm spring-form cake tin and line the base with non-stick baking paper.

Mix the biscuit crumbs and melted butter and press into cake tin. Refrigerate for 15 minutes.

Make a smooth paste with cornflour and water and set aside.

Mix cream cheese in food processor until smooth. Place rest of ingredients in with the cream cheese and process until well combined, lastly adding the cornflour paste and mixing for a further few minutes.

Pour the mixture onto the base and bake for 1¼ hours or until set.

Refrigerate until cold and slice to serve.

Makes 1 x 20 cm cake

INDEX

ACKNOWLEDGEMENTS

The words 'Thank you' seem too small to express my gratitude to the people who take an idea for a book and help to make it a reality. This is my third cookbook, the latest in my Dulcie May-inspired journey, and once again it has taken many people to bring it to fruition.

To my family: thank you for helping me to channel my love of people and food into a product that represents us all. You are committed to my food store in Mt Eden while I create these books and it is incredible for me to know that you have embraced that responsibility. Dulcie May is truly a family effort.

To my sister Michelle: you make these projects run so smoothly. Your dedication and belief in these projects mean the world to me and you truly are a rock for me during busy times.

To Todd: thank you again for capturing my vision and sharing ideas on how to attain it. You are extremely passionate about what you do and I am looking forward to working with you again in the future.

To the team at HarperCollins: thank you for looking forward to the future, believing in me and assisting me to create another beautiful book. You are always open to my ideas and happy to work alongside me to bring them to reality.

Like my previous books, this one would not have been possible without the everyday support of my husband Adam and our daughter Gabby. You are selfless and patient and willing to sacrifice some of our time together as a family for me to pursue my dream. I thank you with all my heart for allowing me to do this. Food and love are made to be shared and I am so grateful to share both of these with you, every day.

Food, family and love form the very essence of who Natalie Oldfield is and where she comes from.

Inspired by her grandmother, Natalie opened her food store Dulcie May Kitchen to coincide with the release of her first, self-published, book *Gran's Kitchen*. Since then, Dulcie May Kitchen has won awards for Best Cake Shop (*Metro* magazine 2009), one of the Top 50 Cafés (*Metro* magazine 2010) as well as Best Pressed Sandwiches (*Metro* magazine 2010). *Gran's Kitchen* also won the renowned Gourmand Book Award in Europe for Best Local Cuisine in New Zealand, and has since been published in Australia and Great Britain. Continuing her Gran's influence of cooking and sharing simple, fresh and flavoursome food, Natalie then published *Gran's Family Table* in 2011.

Loving food as she does, Natalie began her career in the hospitality industry and continues to share her love of food, and people, through her store Dulcie May Kitchen. For more information about Dulcie May Kitchen go to www.dulciemaykitchen.com.